Travis Elborough

The Pocket Essential

NIETZSCHE

www.pocketessentials.com

First published in Great Britain 2001 by Pocket Essentials, 18 Coleswood Road, Harpenden, Herts, AL5 1EQ

Distributed in the USA by Trafalgar Square Publishing, PO Box 257, Howe Hill Road, North Pomfret, Vermont 05053

A CIP catalogue record for this book is available from the British Library.

ISBN 1-903047-49-8

9 8 7 6 5 4 3 2 1

Book typeset by Pdunk
Printed and bound by Cox & Wyman

For Lauren

Acknowledgements

My thanks to the inimitable Nick Rennison and Mr. Ion Mills without whom..., Declan Clarke, Rachel Bailey, Pele Cox and Chris Warne for their advice and encouragement, Alex Mayor and all at the House of Baxendale for their technical support and swinging electro pop beats, Arantxa, Claire Milburn and Herr Shephard for tolerating my rambling conversation, the folks without whom... and everyone at the North London Nietzsche Society, Bull and Last Branch.

CONTENTS

1. Introduction

'Listen to me! For I am thus and thus. Do not, above all, confound me with what I am not!'

Nietzsche, *Ecce Homo*

It is now over a hundred years since the death of the philosopher Friedrich Nietzsche, yet his ideas continue to be controversial. Few thinkers have inspired such differing opinions or such a diverse range of disciples. Nazis, Postmodernists, Socialists, Feminists, Existentialists, Queer-theorists and devotees of physical culture all claim to have been influenced by his work. In the face of such divergent interpretations it can seem difficult to understand exactly what Nietzsche is really all about. This compact guide aims to provide a chance to get to grips with the life and work of a thinker, often considered too mad, bad or dangerous to get to know. During his own lifetime he was largely ignored or misunderstood. After his death he was difficult to ignore but largely misinterpreted- a cruel fate for a thinker so concerned about his intellectual legacy. Part of the blame can be laid on his sinister anti-Semitic sister, Elisabeth, who did much to distort Nietzsche's writings to reflect her own unsavoury views, so donating (by proxy) his intellectual support to National Socialism. But part of the problem also stems from Nietzsche's unique style. He can be polemical, contradictory, abusive, offensive, ironical and even, believe it or not, very witty. Much of his work resists literal readings. He adopts different prose styles, speaks through characters and even changes his mind from one book to the next. This is not, at least traditionally, how many philosophers went about presenting their ideas. Nietzsche is however, not a traditional thinker. He was a professor of philology, the study of the comparative aspects of ancient texts and languages, and the pre-Socratic thinkers, who enjoyed the intellectual challenge of a debate more than actually providing enduring conclusions, had a profound influence on his work. Nietzsche spent most of his tragic life longing to live in, or failing that, to recreate the world of the Ancient Greeks. For though his critiques of religion, science and morality anticipated, shaped and continue to shape our understanding of what it is to be a human being today, he had nothing but contempt for the modern world (one suspects he would not have been that impressed by the postmodern one either). He is a thinker who defies clumsy classifications and spurns reassuring answers and is all the more enjoyable and stimulating for it.

2. The Early Years

The Son Of A Preacher Man

Friedrich Wilhelm Nietzsche was born in 1844, sharing a birthday, October 15th, with the Prussian King Frederick William IV, a fact he did not fail to mention in his autobiography *Ecce Homo*. His father Karl was a Lutheran pastor and the family then lived in the village of Rocken, in the Prussian province of Saxony, near Leipzig. Parsonry was practically the family business. There were at least twenty clergymen in the Nietzsche clan within five generations and his paternal grandfather, Friedrich August Ludwig had been granted an honorary doctorate for his work *Gamaliel*, a spirited defence of Christianity. It was expected that young Friedrich, as the first born male of this particular branch, would follow in their footsteps. Such an aim became an imperative when his father died suddenly of what is recorded as a 'softening of the brain' - one of those handy catch-all nineteenth century diagnoses that seemed to cover every social embarrassing disease from syphilis to congenital deformity - following a fall. Nietzsche was just five at the time and with the death of his baby brother, Joseph, just a few months later, he became the main object of his mother Franziska's attention and the sole focus of her ambitions.

The family moved to Naumburg and there his mother, younger sister Elisabeth, grandmother Erdmuthe, and two aunts, Rosalie and Augusta, raised him in an atmosphere of almost suffocating piety. Doted on and petted the boy, affectionately known as Fritz, grew into a gifted if somewhat henpecked young man, never happier than when quietly reading the bible or writing little poems or performing self-penned plays and songs with Elisabeth and a china squirrel they had christened King Squirrel I. The siblings were very close and the pair shared a bedroom until Nietzsche was twelve. Elisabeth or Lama (Nietzsche's nickname for his sister) adored her brother and from an early age she tried to keep nearly every thing he wrote. This was not an easy task given that Fritz was already a discerning critic of his own work and would often attempt to destroy creations that failed to live up to his standards.

Initially schooled at a local Gymnasium, where his school mates delighted in calling him 'the little minister', he was fourteen when he won a scholarship to attend Schulpforta, a prestigious boarding school. His Pforta medical report still survives and here he is described as 'a robust compact human being with a noticeably fixed look in his eyes, short-sighted and often troubled by shifting headaches.' It goes on to mention his father's unfortunate early demise before adding, rather ominously, that there are 'no bad symptoms yet, but the antecedents should be taken into account.'

At first the teenager found life at his new school hard. Pforta, formed at the time of the Reformation, took education very seriously indeed. Discipline, in the most Spartan sense of the word, was the order of the day. Pupils were roused at the uncivilised hour of 4am and they had lessons, with only a highly regimented break for lunch, until about 8pm. The curriculum, which boasted generous doses of physical exercise, was heavily biased toward Latin and Greek, with ten hours of the former and six hours of the latter every week. Nietzsche proved a star pupil in the classics, which was just as well because his performance in some of the other disciplines was distinctly below par. One now famous story claims that the examiners were supposed to be on the point of failing him when one, presumably his Latin master, exclaimed: 'But gentlemen are we really going to fail the best pupil Pforta has ever had?'

Nietzsche did not however, limit his creative output to the rigid curriculum. With his friends Wilhelm Pinder and Gustav Krug he formed a literary and musical society that they named Germania. The three would discuss poetry, art, music and politics and perform their own compositions. It was at one of these gatherings that Krug, already an avid fan of Richard Wagner, introduced Nietzsche to the piano score to Wagner's *Tristan and Isolde*. Friedrich, whose favourite composer during his school years was the more restrained romantic Schumann, was rather a slow convert. However, during the holidays of 1862, he and Gustav took to playing a bombastic arrangement of this rousing piece from morning until night.

It was also around this time that Nietzsche began to have serious doubts about his faith. Encouraged by his philological classes he began to take a much more questioning approach to reading the scriptures. With puberty now in full flow he was also finding it harder to endure the school's regime. He responded by rebelling in the time-honoured fashion; he became infatuated with one of his sister's friends, wrote some terrible poetry, fell in with a bad crowd and began staying up late drinking. On one occasion he was discovered drunk by one of the teachers. Embarrassed by the punishment - he was stripped of his status as a prefect - he settled down to complete his dissertation in Latin on the sixth-century Greek poet Theognis of Megara without troubling the school's report book any further.

The day after his twentieth birthday he enrolled at the University of Bonn as a student of theology and philology. It is highly likely that by this stage he had already abandoned the idea of a career in the church but felt compelled by the wishes

11

of his mother and sister to continue studying theology. In the meantime he set about enjoying the more relaxed atmosphere of university life and even joined Franconia, a student drinking fraternity with vaguely patriotic political leanings.

1865 proved to be a formative year for Nietzsche in more ways than one. In February of that year he visited Cologne. According to the account he gave to his friend Paul Deussen he asked a porter to take him to a restaurant. Either the porter misheard him or he assumed that hunger was not the only appetite that needed satisfying because the student found himself escorted to a brothel. Trying to make the best of the situation Nietzsche claimed he suddenly noticed there was a piano there and so played a few short pieces, made some excuses and left. His account convinced Deussen. Others including Thomas Mann, who dramatised the moment in his novel *Doctor Faustus*, are not so sure. Did he go back? Was the piano the only thing he played with? Did he visit other brothels? No one can be entirely certain.

When he returned home at Easter his family found him quite different. He refused to attend the Easter services and announced that he was going to give up studying theology. Elisabeth was devastated. Over the following months she wrote to him exhorting him to change his mind. Fritz replied, effectively spelling out his creed, 'If you want peace of mind and happiness, then have faith; if you want to be a disciple of truth, then search.'

In August he left Bonn and followed his philology tutor Albrecht Ritschl to the University of Leipzig. A few months later he was browsing in a second-hand bookshop in the city when he stumbled on a neglected looking volume by Arthur Schopenhauer called *The World as Will and Representation*. Within days of reading it Nietzsche proudly announced to his friends he had become a Schopenhauerian.

Uncle Arthur

What exactly was it about Arthur Schopenhauer's philosophy that so enchanted Nietzsche? There is nothing more suited to the teenage mind than gloom – as the appeal of The Smiths and Slipknot shows today - and Schopenhauer positively revels in misery. When Nietzsche stumbled on his work, the Danzig-born thinker had been dead for just over five years and although he had enjoyed a modicum of fame during the last seven years of life, few thinkers seemed more willing to embrace the grave. If Leibniz held that this world was the best of all possible worlds, Schopenhauer argued it would always be the worst of all possible worlds. His grim outlook appears to have formed early in life. His mercantile father had forced him to pursue a business apprenticeship and at seventeen he claimed to have been 'gripped by the misery of life'. His own academic career was only possible after his father's death, itself an act of suicide. While this death was certainly fortuitous for Arthur, he blamed and resented his mother for her part in his father's demise and then for her subsequent fame as a novelist. Perhaps unsurprisingly his writings are littered with scathing attacks on women. Schopenhauer did not restrict his attacks to the printed page and once pushed a seamstress who had disturbed him down the stairs, injuring her permanently.

The completion of his magnum opus, *The World As Will and Representation*, was met with unanimous indifference (a fate that befell Nietzsche's work during his sane lifetime) but it did gain him an assistant position at the university of Berlin. Here he rather foolishly decided to schedule his own lectures at the same time as those of Hegel, then seen as the inheritor of both Kant's philosophy and his esoteric terminology. Schopenhauer's failure to seduce students away from

Germany's most renowned idealist led him to renounce lecturing forever. This decision is typical of both his arrogance and the steely determination with which he conducted his life. While his writings may have advocated renouncing the horrors of existence his daily routine seemed to show little signs of adhering to such doctrines. Each morning he would leave the seclusion of his Frankfurt home to read *The Times* in the public library. Later he would embark on a walk, regardless of the weather, before indulging in an evening of flute playing or attending the theatre. Guests would have to quickly adapt to such rituals or receive a brush with his well-developed temper. However, despite such a stony façade, Schopenhauer had something of a reputation as a witty conversationalist.

Schopenhauer's philosophy, like that of so many of the contemporaries he despised, begins by espousing many of the metaphysical conventions conceived by Kant. Immanuel Kant held that the everyday world, the world given in sense-perception, is ideal, mere representation, a creation of the human mind quite different from the reality or 'world-in-itself' that underlies it. As a biological survival mechanism the human brain presents the world to us in a useful way rather than a way coincidental with underlying reality. We have to experience the world in time and space, we have to experience causal connections which persist through time. So it follows that, if objects must exist in space and in time for us to experience them, we must also be enduring mental substances. Schopenhauer, unlike the idealists who chose to abandon Kant's troublesome concept of the thing-in-itself in favour of a world of pure ideas, believed we could form ideas about the true nature of things-in-themselves. This for him was possible because we not only experience the phenomenal world through space and time but as a body. We therefore experience ourselves not only like other external objects of perception but also from within as a will to live. It is this will that is the primal reality of our universe. It is outside of time and space and all reason is subject to what he sees as its pernicious striving.

So, while the everyday phenomenal world is made up of individuals, the metaphysical reality, 'the will' beneath, is beyond plurality ie. one singular entity. It is this illusion of difference that leads us to experience the world as an evil, viciously competitive place. We are therefore compelled by the character of existence to cause one another suffering. The will has only one goal, that of perpetuating its very existence and Schopenhauer's state of nature, much like that of the English philosopher Thomas Hobbes, is a state of perpetual conflict. (This primacy of the life-force or 'will' is maintained by Nietzsche but, as we shall see, in his mature philosophy he transforms it into the life-affirming 'Will to Power.')

For Schopenhauer it is only through aesthetic contemplation that we can escape this dreadful reality. True works of art offer us rare moments of metaphysical insight and penetrate, to use Schopenhauer's Upanishad-inspired phrase, the 'veil of Maya'. We realise that we are not individuals but part of a universal whole and cease, briefly, to strive. He feels that the noblest form of art is tragedy, because through it we become most keenly aware of the 'supersensible side of our nature'. Another key element that certainly would have appealed to the young Nietzsche is the special place music has in Schopenhauer's philosophical system. For while the other arts offer us representations of individuals or events of reality that provide insights into the will, music gives us an immediate copy of the will. He derives this view from music's immediate and seemingly abstract character. Opera becomes problematic for Schopenhauer, as it seems imply that the purest form of music is instrumental, and it is with some reluctance that this Rossini-loving thinker states that opera is 'an unmusical invention for the benefit of unmusical minds'.

While art can offer us welcome respite from the striving of the will, Schopenhauer contends that it is only through embracing a Buddhist rejection of life that we can find peace. Some would contend, though notably not Nietzsche, that suicide would appear to be a more appropriate course of action but for Schopenhauer this is not an enlightened form of rejection. It is just the will asserting its insidious aims again.

In The Army Now

If reading Schopenhauer proved to be a life-changing intellectual and emotional experience for Nietzsche it did not, at least for the next couple of years, disturb his academic career. With a first publication under his belt he had become Albrecht Ritschl's star pupil. Unfortunately for Nietzsche his nation had other plans for him and he found himself duly conscripted to do a year's national service with the mounted section of the Prussian field artillery. A fine philologist he might have been but a horseman he was not and, after being badly injured in a riding accident, he spent most of his time confined to his sick bed before finally being discharged from duty. He returned to Leipzig and there, in late October of 1868, he happened to attend a performance of Wagner's Tristan and Meistersinger preludes. Like the discovery of Schopenhauer, this was a revelation to Nietzsche and by chance he found himself meeting the great composer just eleven days later.

Dick Dastardly

In October 1868, Richard Wagner had returned to his native city, Leipzig, in order to visit his sister Ottilie and her husband Herman Brockhaus. Wagner was still a controversial figure at the time. His involvement in the failed revolutionary uprising in Dresden during 1849 had resulted in his exile from Germany for over ten years. Although he was granted a partial amnesty in 1860 it wasn't until 1862 that he was finally granted leave to visit Saxony. In the same year he settled in Vienna but, two years later, had to flee the city to avoid mounting debts. Luckily Ludwig II, then only 18 years old and already showing an enthusiasm for fairytale style castles and for Wagner's *Lohengrin*, had just been crowned King of Bavaria. Ludwig paid off his debts, installed the composer in a sumptuous villa in Munich and provided him with financial support from the public purse. Unfortunately, just a year later, the King was forced to banish Wagner to Tribschen in Switzerland following an outcry from the good burghers of Munich over his frivolous spending habits and his extramarital cohabitation with Cosima von Bulow, the daughter of Liszt and then the wife of the city's brilliant musical director, Hans von Bulow. Although technically free to visit Saxony when he liked, the unwelcome attentions of the press and his legion of creditors made moving around extremely difficult for Wagner. When he returned to Leipzig that autumn he stayed strictly incognito, letting only family and close friends know he was in town. Fortunately for Nietzsche the wife of his tutor, Sophie Ritschl, was on intimate terms with Ottilie Brockhaus and when Wagner arrived she was introduced to him. Wagner, who delighted in holding court, played her his Meisterlied composition. Frau Ritschl mentioned that she was familiar with the piece because one of her husband's pupils was something of an admirer of his music. Wagner, never one to pass up the chance of meeting a fan, asked if he could meet the young student.

Nietzsche was duly summoned. When he arrived at the Wagner house he found that the composer had gone out, wearing 'an immense hat', probably intended to hide his identity but more than likely only drawing attention to it. Friedrich decided not to scour the streets of Leipzig looking for a gentleman in outsize headgear. Instead he accepted an invitation to return on the following evening, a Sunday. Nietzsche, imagining evening dress essential, then visited his tailor who promised to have a suit ready for him in time for the meeting. Nietzsche spent most of the next day in an agitated state waiting for his suit. It was half past six in the evening before the tailor's assistant finally materialised. The assistant had the suit but he also had a bill and refused to give up the clothing unless he received payment. Nietzsche was exasperated. He didn't have the money in his room, if he had it at all. He grabbed the suit and began to get dressed. Unfortunately the future advocate of the will to power proved no match for the assistant who quickly wrestled it from Nietzsche's grasp and made off with it into the night. Nietzsche, now fearing he would be late, put his old black jacket back on and headed out after him.

When he arrived he was relieved to discover an informal and intimate gathering. Only his friend Windisch, members of the Brockhaus family and the great man himself were present. He was introduced and he and the composer spent a great deal of time talking about Schopenhauer. Wagner regaled the party with anecdotes about his own student days in Leipzig and played them sections from his Meistersinger on the piano. At the end of the evening he invited Nietzsche to visit him so they could make music and discuss philoso-

18

phy. Just a few months later a new job would allow Nietzsche not only to follow up this initial offer but also to become a regular and valued visitor to Wagner's Swiss home in Tribschen.

The Little Professor

Friedrich Nietzsche, on the recommendation of Ritschl, was made the chair of classical philology at Basel University in the spring of 1869. He was just 24 and was awarded his doctorate from Leipzig without having to trifle with exams. The post, which came with the right be addressed as Professor Extraordinarius, did require Nietzsche to become a Swiss citizen. Prussia was still in political turmoil and the university authorities were worried that if he were called on for military service it would interfere with his academic duties. Nietzsche got as far as renouncing his Prussian citizenship but never actually completed all the requirements to become a fully-fledged member of the Swiss nation. In fact, rather fittingly, he remained stateless for the rest of his days. He had been in Basel less than a month when he decided to visit Wagner. Their second meeting proved to be such a success that Nietzsche was invited to attend the Master's 56th birthday party. Unable to attend he wrote a sickeningly fawning letter proclaiming Wagner as Schopenhauer's spiritual brother. When he did return to Tribschen his stay coincided with the birth of Richard and Cosima's first son. Wagner saw this as a good omen and it was not long before Nietzsche was virtually one of the family. (Cod-Freudians will have already noticed that Wagner, 31 years Nietzsche's senior, was old enough to be his father.)

The Disorderly Orderly

With the outbreak of the Franco-Prussian War in July 1870, Nietzsche, no doubt to the annoyance of his University, applied to become a medical orderly for the Prussian army. As in his previous brush with military life, he was not particularly helpful to the Prussian cause. He managed to contract dysentery and diphtheria while treating the troops and wound up in one of the very military hospitals he was supposed to be working in.

Back In Basel

By the time the Prussian-led North German Confederation finally overwhelmed France in January 1871, Nietzsche was back in Basel and hard at work on the book he hoped would make his name. Just a few months earlier he had written to his friend Erwin Rohde expressing his desire to break with philology in order to put himself more fully at Wagner's disposal. The composer had now begun to raise the capital for his long-dreamed-of festival theatre in Bayreuth and Nietzsche appears to have been willing even to give up his career to help him. As it was, he decided to remain in academia. Yet it would, in effect, be Wagner's (as well as Schopenhauer's) influence that would ultimately destroy his reputation as a scholar.

The Birth Of Tragedy

As the youngest and brightest professor of philology of the time Nietzsche's first book was eagerly awaited in the academic world. It would be an understatement to say that *The Birth of Tragedy* was not exactly what was expected. Dedicated to Richard Wagner, it could scarcely be described as a work of philology at all and shortly after it was published in 1872 another young philologist Ulrich Wilamowitz-Moellendorff viciously attacked the book, denouncing what he felt was its lack of scholarship.

He failed to notice that Nietzsche had left the world of philology far behind him. He was attempting to solve what he saw as the crisis in German culture, give an account of Greek tragedy, re-write the history of metaphysics and come up with a convincing new theory of aesthetics. Oh, yes... and praise Wagner to the skies.

The fundamental aim of the book was to answer one, not very, simple question. In the light of Schopenhauer's pessimism, how were we to affirm life? Nietzsche, schooled at a shrine to the ancient world and a Professor of classics, rather unsurprisingly, thought the Greeks could give us a few clues. The Greeks were no strangers to the sheer awfulness of life yet he felt through tragedy they had found a way not only to reconcile themselves to life but also to revel in it.

Schopenhauer, as we have seen, also saw tragedy as the noblest form of art. It was only through encountering great aesthetic works that we became aware of ourselves not as individuals but as part of a metaphysical unity and could cease the competitive striving that was the scourge of existence. Nietzsche wondered if realising you were part of a universal whole might have darker consequences. If you came to view yourself as part of metaphysical oneness you could start to regard others as valueless and dispensable. You might be at the mercy of a 'horrible witches' brew' of sensuality and cruelty. He saw Schopenhauer's concept of 'the will' as being like Dionysus, the Greek god of wine, intoxication and revelry. Festivals similar in style to those of Dionysus took place in cultures around the world and throughout history. Nietzsche is at pains to differentiate those of the Greeks from all others. The latter he feels were little more than barbaric, drunken shagathons. The Greeks had Apollo, the god of order, reason and illusion, on hand to prevent them from embracing the more feverish aspects of the festivities.

It is this combination of Dionysus and Apollo that, Nietzsche claimed, gives Greek tragedy its power. The Apollinian sense of oneself as a contemplative individual is not shocked by the Dionysian. It is, on the contrary, enriched. The audiences would be captivated and then united by the chorus, allowing the Apollinian individuals to share in a Dionysian community where life, replete with all its horrors, could be celebrated. 'It is only as an aesthetic phenomenon', Nietzsche argued, 'that existence and the world are eternally justified.' Tragedy was a way of imbuing the world with value. The value of myths.

If Ancient Greek tragedy was such a potent force for good what one, might wonder went wrong? Nietzsche points the finger of blame at the dramatist Euripides. Under the pernicious influence of Socrates, Euripides had destroyed tragedy by reducing the role of the chorus. In doing so he tipped the balance of future plays and Greek culture towards the Apollinian. Reason, not art, had thus been allowed to dominate. From then on western culture had repressed Dionysus, becoming sick in the process. Socrates had sowed the seeds for the theology of the Christian church and duped philosophers and scientists ever since into believing they could discover absolute truths. Unfortunately for them Kant had exposed the limits of rationality. He had, as described earlier, proposed that the human brain presented the world to us in a useful way and that the world as we perceived it was quite different from the reality or 'world-in-itself' that underlies it. The optimism of rationalism was doomed to failure because there were only certain things human beings would ever discover. Nietzsche thought it was high time we learnt, once more, to be a little more honest about what being a human really meant. Only by accepting our mortality, i.e. the essentially pessimistic vision of the Dionysian, could we repair the damage of two thousand years of cultural disease and decay.

There are no prizes for guessing who, in late 19th century Germany, Nietzsche suggested was most able to assist in this cultural rebirth. Richard Wagner, with his operatic versions of German myths, was, Nietzsche argued, synthesising the Apollinian and Dionysian principles. Where Kant and Schopenhauer had made it possible for the spirit of Germany philosophy to destroy Socrates, Wagner's music would redeem and revitalise German culture.

Wagner, as we can imagine, was immensely pleased with the book. Very few others were. There is evidence to suggest that while Nietzsche was keen to promote the composer's cause he did not initially intend the book to include the undiluted paean to Wagner that appears in the latter half. The first draft confined itself to exploring the origins of Greek tragedy and most who read it, and later Nietzsche himself, wished he'd done just that. The Greeks were to remain the one cause Nietzsche would never abandon. At the time though Wagner's enthusiastic reaction was enough to convince him he was on the right track and a few months later he fought off shingles to attend the laying of the foundation stone at Bayreuth.

Nietzsche, as we have seen even from his school medical report, was a sickly child. As a grown man his health did not improve. Military service had hospitalised him twice and whilst writing *The Birth of Tragedy* he had been plagued by illness. The book's obsession with the decay of culture looks inspired, or the very least coloured by, his poor health. From 1871 onwards he waged a constant battle against raging headaches and nausea.

In 1950 Walter Kaufman, who did much to popularise Nietzsche's thought after the war and who is still regarded by many as one of the finest translators of his work, claimed that perhaps Nietzsche had contracted syphilis 'through a skin wound during the war when he ministered sick soldiers' and that this is what so severely altered his health. While this is plausible from a medical point of view, we now know that Nietzsche sought treatment for syphilitic infections twice in 1867. There is certainly no doubt that he had the 'French pox' but his doctors may not have informed him of the nature of his illness. How he caught the disease remains unanswered. Did he catch it 'playing the piano' in the brothel he visited as a student? Or, given his longstanding record of migraines, did he inherit it from his father who had died from a strange 'brain-softening' ailment? The latter is something that Nietzsche himself alludes to in a letter to Franz Overbeck in 1888 - though he rather euphemistically describes his ill health as being caused by inheriting his father's 'lack of stamina'.

Wagner Is Waning

In the summer of 1873 Nietzsche began to give a series of lectures on Pre-Socratic philosophy. Ironically, for someone who had just lambasted Socrates in print, his lecturing style owed a great deal to the dialogues of Socrates's great pupil, Plato. Paul Ree, an equally precocious and pioneering young scholar, attended the lectures. Ree, who was beginning to use psychology to answer philosophical questions, proved to be a decisive influence on Nietzsche and not least in his views about Wagner.

With Richard and Cosima now in Bayreuth, Nietzsche had a greater time to reflect on his future and, although he was still actively involved in raising money for the festival, his enthusiasm appeared to have cooled. His own work and his friendship with Ree were not only taking him further away from philology but also from Wagner. When Nietzsche made what was to be his last visit to the Wagners' new home, Wahnfried, in August 1874 he took with him something unusual, at least unusual in Wagnerian circles. Wagner hated Brahms. To admit to liking any other German composer at all was to invoke his wrath but his contempt for Brahms, the man and his music, was without bounds. So for Nietzsche to arrive at Wahnfried with the piano score for Brahms' *Triumphlied* tucked under his arm and then to leave it on Wagner's piano was an act of sedition. Catching sight of it Wagner resorted to his customary technique for settling disputes: he ranted and shouted. Nietzsche just sulked. Although the pair continued to correspond, they did not see each other for the next two years.

Out Of Time

Usually translated in English as either *Untimely Meditations* or, the more jolly sounding, *Thoughts Out Of Season*, Nietzsche's next book comprised four longish essays published over three years. They illustrated just how difficult it was for him to resolve his feelings about Wagner and Schopenhauer. The first essay, an attack on the rational humanist David Strauss, was virtually written at Wagner's request. Strauss, a former theologian who had abandoned his faith to become a leading advocate of a form of Darwinian German patriotism, had publicly denounced Wagner's influence on Ludwig II some years before. Wagner, never one to give up a grudge, encouraged Nietzsche to attack Strauss' latest book. This he did quite convincingly. Though in many respects Strauss' views on religion were not a million miles from his own, Nietzsche was staggered to discover how sloppily the text was written and then became enraged by Strauss' failure to grasp the true meaning of atheism. Without God, Nietzsche argued, there was no point clinging to old morality. If Darwin was right the whole conception of the world had to change. Ethics, at least in the Judaeo-Christian sense that Strauss assumed would prevail, might not be possible at all. If such an attack wasn't enough to destroy the book, he concluded with over seventy examples of grammatical and stylistic offences that Nietzsche felt were an insult to the German language. (Most English editions choose to omit this section on the grounds that it loses its potency in translation.) David Strauss died six months after the essay was published. Whether his end was speeded by such a vicious assault we can only speculate but the issue appears to have played on Nietzsche's mind because he wrote to his friend Carl von Gersdoff saying, 'I very much hope I did not sadden his last months.' In art he might well be the devil incarnate but, in life, Nietzsche was almost peculiarly considerate.

The next essay, 'On the uses and disadvantages of history', is by far the most interesting in the collection. However, let's briefly examine the last two first. 'Schopenhauer as educator' is a peculiar piece. It is interesting in that it claims that the old pessimist has a 'cheerfulness that really cheers' but it is largely an unfocussed attempt by Nietzsche to define the concept of the true genius. Schopenhauer, he concludes, is such a man because he had intellectual courage and rejected the academic community of his day. No doubt Nietzsche had his own situation firmly in mind as he wrote. 'Richard Wagner in Bayreuth' was conceived along the same lines but, following their little spat in Wahnfried, Nietzsche appears, and certainly writes as if he is, less committed to the Wagnerian cause. Though the final version is less critical than the first draft, it still displays the tensions in Nietzsche's relationship with the composer.

'On the uses and disadvantages of history' is rather different; here in embryonic form we find many of the ideas that would preoccupy Nietzsche during his post-Wagner period.

'History', Henry Ford claimed was, 'just bunk' and in many respects Nietzsche would have been inclined to agree with him. For Nietzsche, unlike many of his contemporaries who he felt seemed to accept the subject as an intrinsic good, history was only valuable if it had a positive effect on life. There is, for Nietzsche, no point to history if it means our necks are bent so far backward we are unable to look forward. History makes the vital present just another episode in a series of events. It inhibits creativity because we feel unable, in the face of the past, to effect the future. We end up being so jaded by the idea of constant flux that we believe the present does not matter. This is a cardinal sin for Nietzsche

27

because we become 'wandering encyclopaedias' with no real idea what our culture is. We merely inherit the unquestioned ideas of the past. If we want to create a truly vibrant culture, he argues, we must either adopt an 'unhistorical' attitude where we accept a limit horizon, learning to forget the weight of history, or embrace the 'suprahistorical', where we only choose to consider history which 'bestows upon existence the character of the eternal', as in art. The suprahistorical is an early version of the concept of 'overcoming' that will lead Nietzsche to formulate the ideas of the overman and the eternal recurrence.

The Truly Detestable Festival

The final break with Wagner was actually far less dramatic than is usually supposed, but was none the less traumatic for Nietzsche. The image of Nietzsche storming out of Bayreuth, unable to stomach Wagner's public display of anti-Semitism, owes more to the zeal of post-Second World War academics, keen to distance the thinker from his reputation as Hitler's favourite philosopher, and the account he himself gives of the occasion in *Ecce Homo*, than to reality. What is certain is that Nietzsche, who attended the festival with his Jewish friend Ree, was certainly shocked to find Wagner strutting around the place like a Teutonic rooster. If, as seems most likely, Nietzsche had already decided his relationship with the composer was almost finished before the festival, Bayreuth then proved to be the final straw.

In the months leading up to the festival savage headaches and stomach cramps had prevented Nietzsche from attending any of the rehearsals. At Christmas 1875 he suffered a complete physical collapse and had to give up teaching for several months. He travelled to Geneva to recuperate. By spring he felt well enough to offer a proposal of marriage to Mathilde Trampedach, a pretty 21-year old whom he had met there. Probably wisely she chose to reject the chance of becoming Mrs. Nietzsche. He returned to Basel and set up home with his sister. The production of *Human, All Too Human,* his first profoundly anti-Wagnerian work was well underway so when he departed for Wagner's ringfest in July there can be little doubt that he was already distancing himself from the composer's ideas.

On the evening Nietzsche arrived public rehearsals of the *Götterdämmerung* were being performed. He attended the first part but, feeling unwell, left before its end. Two days later a severe pain in his eyes meant he could only listen to a performance of *Die Walküre*. He spent a few days resting in the Bavarian Forest and returned for the official opening on August 12th.

What confronted him looked more like a fusion between the appalling and the disastrous than the Apollinian and the Dionysian. In scenes closer to farce than tragedy, Wotan managed to lose *the* ring in *Das Rheingold* and the mechanical dragon for *Siegfried* looked ludicrous. The dragon had been built in England and transported to Bayreuth piece by piece. Somehow the neck had got lost and so the poor beast was forced to appear with its head attached directly on to its shoulders. If the events on the stage were a disaster, the audience were even worse. Nietzsche could only look around him in horror at the braying anti-Semitic multitude that Wagner appeared to have gathered around him. Wagner's home had, Nietzsche felt, become a drop-in centre for bored and unmusical nobility who treated the whole event as if it was nothing more than a day at the races. He avoided the composer and the second cycle of *Das Rheingold* and left with Ree on August 27th.

On returning to Basel ill health once again reappeared and Nietzsche was granted a year off by the university. He went to Italy with Ree and the young novelist Albert Brenner and, by chance, bumped into Wagner. They met several times here and, like the old days, seemed to have a number of long talks. Wagner was working on *Parsifal*, Nietzsche on *Human, All Too Human*. These would be the last times they met. For Nietzsche *Parsifal*, a piece about religious redemption, was nothing short a betrayal of all he hoped Wagner had been capable. Wagner's music was supposed to be the cultural redeemer and yet here he was proposing Christian resignation. To Nietzsche this was unthinkable. When Wagner was sent a copy of *Human, All To Human*, the composer took it as ample proof that Friedrich's mind had finally cracked. In a letter he claimed to have 'done him (Nietzsche) the kindness of not reading his book and my greatest wish and hope is that one day he will thank us for this.' Shortly after *Human All Too Human* was published Nietzsche suffered his worst and most protracted migraine and in June of 1879 he retired from Basel University on a small pension.

3. The Middle Years

New Style Nietzsche

Human All Too Human marks the end of Nietzsche's enchantment not only with Wagner but also with the romanticism that, stylistically and intellectually, shaped *The Birth of Tragedy* and *Thoughts Out of Season*. The Greeks still get a look in here and there, of course, but Nietzsche had put away such childish things as metaphysics and gone on to embrace science.

Dedicated to the arch French rationalist Voltaire (a dedication removed when it was republished in 1886) and with a quote from Descartes extolling the joy of reason on the first page, *Human, All Too Human* left little doubt that Nietzsche had changed his tack. Many of his friends, the Wagners particularly, were horrified. Most held the psychologist, Paul Ree, responsible. Unlike Wagner, who had been rather a forbidding and formidable mentor to Nietzsche, Ree was a peer and it is obvious that he enjoyed the freedom of being able to discuss ideas on an equal footing. Ree was an atheist who felt that belief in god was a subjective phenomenon i.e. the result of human psychology rather than the objective existence of a deity. He also maintained that morality was a matter of custom rather than nature. These ideas chimed with Nietzsche's own views about the state of existence in the post-Darwinian world. It was also at Ree's suggestion that Nietzsche became acquainted with the work of the French aphorist La Rochefoucauld. At the time most of his compatriots held aphorisms in low esteem, so Nietzsche's conscious decision to embrace a very Gallic form of writing was another sign of his rejection of Wagner and his German ideals.

In the longish aphorism Nietzsche had also discovered a form ideally suited to his style of thinking. With ill health now a constant he was often restricted to short bursts of activity. If he did know the true nature of his disease, he would also have known he only had a limited time to complete his work. He did most of his thinking whilst out walking and there is something peripatetic about his style from *Human, All Too Human* onwards. The aphorism allowed him to dash ideas down without laboriously spelling out each stage of the arguments. 'Most thinkers,' he claimed, 'write badly because they tell us not only their thoughts but also the thinking of the thoughts'. From now on Nietzsche wouldn't be one of these.

The book is fundamentally concerned with material, psychological and social truth. Nietzsche begins by reasserting Kant's view that the world as it appears to us is constructed by human faculties and that the mysterious world in-itself that supposedly lies behind it is both unknowable and inconsequential. Our urge to posit both this metaphysical netherworld and god must be down to human psychology. Anticipating the work of philosophers such as Wittgenstein, he goes on to argue that with language man erroneously assumed that s/he was not just giving labels to things but s/he was expressing a higher knowledge of them. Through language we believed we had discovered the eternal truths of the world, forgetting that language itself was a human invention and therefore a cultural phenomenon.

Moralists had also made the mistake; morality was not inherent in or determined by reality. 'Good' and 'evil' were not expressions of God-given eternal truths but social constructions. Morality varied from culture to culture and throughout history. In the good old days of Ancient Greece the strong, conquering spirit was admirable whereas in Christian societies meekness came to be regarded as good.

(Nietzsche, unsurprisingly, preferred the Greek model.) What we feel as conscience is in fact the values of the community that were drummed into us as children. Freud would develop a similar theory with his notion of the superego.

The notion of power is extremely important for Nietzsche. Power, for him, is an essential part of our psychology. In Greek culture, he tells us, brute power was virtually equated with goodness. It was 'not the man who inflicts harm on us but the man who is contemptible' that was considered bad. It was in the Judaeo-Christian world that the oppressed, power-less ones came to regard the actions of the strong as bad and their actions evil. Yet this too he feels is an expression of the desire for power. In reworking St Luke he claims that 'He who humbles himself wants to be exulted.' For Nietzsche even actions, like humility, that on the surface don't seem to driven by the urge for power, are equally manifestations of it. This tendency has its most extreme form in that of the saint. Ascetics, loving power but lacking others to dominate, effectively tyrannise themselves. The idea of exerting power over oneself is essential to the concept of the Superman or Over-man and his descriptions of the roots of morality are developed further in *The Genealogy of Morals*.

I Prefer To See Things This Way

Human, All Too Human is the first full expression of what is usually referred to as Nietzsche's perspectivism. As we have seen he denies the idea of an objective truth. Each perspective is an equally valid interpretation of the world. He does, however, believe that truths are possible and what he calls free spirits - those willing to question the assumptions of society i.e. thinkers like himself - will be able to find them. It could be argued that on the grounds of his own theory this is also just another perspective and, as such, no more likely to true. Probably Nietzsche would have claimed his work was just interpretation and was open to the same criticism as any other.

Have Thoughts Will Travel

Free from academic life but still ailing, Nietzsche spent the latter part of 1879 recuperating in Switzerland and writing *The Wanderer and His Shadow*, a supplement to *Human, All Too Human*. He returned to Naumburg where he claimed he was going to give up thinking and concentrate on gardening. It wasn't long before both thinking and travelling were back on the agenda. The pattern of drifting from place to place was established in the first few years after he left the University and, for the remainder of his sane life, he lived in hotels and lodging rooms in Germany, Switzerland and Italy.

1880 was reasonably productive for Nietzsche. He completed *Daybreak*, a book that expanded and developed the critique of Christian morality that had appeared in *Human, All Too Human*. However, he was crippled by headaches and stomach cramps for most of the following year and he found it extremely difficult to think, let alone write. After a few unpleasant months in Italy, visiting his friend and disciple the composer Paul Gast, he travelled to the Engadine in south-eastern Switzerland. Here in August 1881 he rented a single-room in a house in Sils-Maria in the Ober-Engadine. It would prove to be his most permanent residence. Nietzsche adored and was inspired by the mountain views and he found the fresh air, warmed just slightly by the region's proximity to Italy, reasonably conducive to his health. He spent seven summers there and penned the majority of his next five books there. It was here while out walking, as he puts it, '6,000 feet beyond man and time', that he first hit upon the ideas of the eternal recurrence and Zarathustra.

Spanish Eyes

The alpine winters were unfortunately too hazardous for Nietzsche's health and by October he retreated to Genoa. If this Italian city lacked the icy grandeur of the Alps its concert hall provided him with a whole new inspiration. The future Good European found himself bowled over by an opera on a Spanish theme by a French composer. Shortly after viewing Bizet's *Carmen* for the second time, he wrote to Peter Gast to report 'he had been very ill, but well as a result of *Carmen*.' Bizet's music was the perfect antithesis to Wagner. Seven years later, after he had seen it for the twentieth time, he claimed each time he heard it made him 'more a philosopher, a better philosopher' and it was with this work that he took leave 'of the damp north, of all the steam of the Wagnerian ideal'.

Carmen liberated Nietzsche from Wagner. Its Latin spirit had a buoyant and disruptive energy. He felt Bizet had unleashed a sensibility previously absent from the music of civilised Europe. In his letter he alluded to the novella by Prosper Merimee on which the opera's libretto is based. If we consider the fact that Merimee's book makes dextrous use of an unreliable narrator (the story of Carmen, the gypsy heroine and Don Jose, her ill-starred dragoon lover, is presented as an aside in a work that is claimed to be a socio- historical study) and of Ovidian myth, Nietzsche's enthusiasm for the opera seems even more understandable.

In Ovid the hunter Actaeon pushes aside the branches so he can see Diana at her bath. He is punished by being turned into a stag and chased by his own dogs. His fate reflects the dangerous price of knowledge; those who hunt may find themselves metamorphosed into the hunted. Carmen like Diana is a deadly temptress and to seek her is to invite madness and death. Jose follows her into a world of smuggling and highway robbery but her free spirit is ultimately too much for him. He lacks the courage and the love to allow her to be truly free and so can only destroy. Carmen is beyond conventional morality. When cards are read, predicting her certain death, she accepts her fate singing 'En vain pour eviter les responses ameres'. (It is in vain to reject their results). She is prepared to die because in life she is never tamed. When the moment arrives she refuses to yield to Jose even though she knows he will kill her. Her defiance is an acceptance of mortality. She dies in effect laughing at the cruel finitude of life. These are all good Nietzschean themes.

The Gay Science

Carmen for Nietzsche symbolised 'the tragic spirit that is the essence of love' and, through it, he had found a new aesthetic ideal. His next book, *The Gay Science*, was enthused by its spirit. In 1888 he described the book as an exploration of the Provencal concept of the 'gaya scienza'. Modern European poetry is descended from the art of the troubadours but when Pope Innocent III annihilated the Cathars early in the thirteenth century, in the Albigensian Crusade, much of their culture was destroyed. The Provencal dialect is closely related to the Occitan language in which troubadour poetry first flowered and during the fourteenth century the *gai saber* or art of poetry was still cultivated in Provence. Occitan and its related dialects Gascon, Limousin and, of course, Provencal are as close to Catalan and Spanish as French. The word

Occitan derives from the phrase *langue d'oc*, literally the language of yes, *oc* and not *oui* being the affirmative in Occitan and her sister dialects. By invoking the Provencal art of poetry Nietzsche is not only cocking a snook at dusty Teutonic methodology he is also revealing his aim to affirm life and look south, to Spain and the Mediterranean, for inspiration.

Both the ideas of the eternal recurrence and the superman make their preliminary appearances in this book but it is one of Nietzsche's most striking and famous pronouncements in a strange parable called 'The Madman' that is most worthy of immediate attention. In a crowded market place a madman with a lamp arrives and, after asking where God has gone, begins to tell the throng that, 'God is dead. God remains dead. And we have killed him' The crowd, many of whom, Nietzsche says, did not believe in God, only look on in astonishment. The madman eventually throws his lamp on the ground and leaves saying, 'I have come too early... my time is not yet... This deed is still more distant from them than the most distant stars- and yet they have done it themselves.' Knowledge of Nietzsche's own descent into madness tends to tempt modern readers of the passage to see it as remarkably prophetic. However, Nietzsche's main concern in this parable is with suggesting the nature of a world that is, in effect, now meaningless.

In *The Birth of Tragedy* Nietzsche thought art could replace God. By the time of *Human, All Too Human* he had rejected this tenet and seemed to feel that science was able to make the world meaningful for us. When he came to write *The Gay Science* he clearly had doubts about the claims of science to keep the horrors of existence at bay. In this parable, and as a recurrent theme in the whole work, he examines the dangers of replacing God with science. The crowd who do not believe in God (clearly intended to represent scientists) still think and act as if God were a reality. The chief offenders, Nietzsche feels, are the Utilitarians who proclaim that science and morality should 'give men as much pleasure and as little displeasure as possible.' Yet all they have done is borrowed a Christian concept without the justification from an absolute power. Their claim to a universal law therefore has no grounds. Science just like religion without a God cannot have an 'absolute value.' This seems to lead Nietzsche very close to nihilism but while he does claim that 'delusion and error are conditions of human knowledge' he believes that by creating our own values the world can have meaning. It is just a case of casting aside the stodgy intellectual hunt for truth and embracing a better, in the sense of life-affirming, wisdom. To do this we must learn to become 'superficial out of profundity.' A gay or cheerful science would be one where we create for ourselves an 'exuberant freedom above things.' We turn both the world and ourselves into aesthetic phenomena. In a phrase that sounds curiously Freudian, except that Nietzsche obviously feels this is beneficial, he says as artists we 'learn to forget well, and to be good at not knowing.' This would sound like the Nietzsche of *The Birth of Tragedy* but, in the earlier book, art was thought to connect us to the metaphysical truth whereas here he sees art as the replacement for truth.

Nietzsche's truth seems remarkably similar to the version adhered to by the perfidious park keepers in the American writer George Saunders' wonderful short story 'Pastoralia'. Truth, for them 'is that thing which empowers us to do even better that we are doing at the moment. So when a rumour makes you doubt us, us up here, it is therefore not true, since we have already defined truth as that thing which helps us win. Therefore, if you want to know what is true simply ask what is best.'

Baby One More Time

Nietzsche obviously found the flight from truth slightly problematic. Despite urging us to embark on a course of giddy gay science he feels compelled to provide us with some metaphorical ballast in the form of the heaviest burden, an early version of the eternal recurrence.

What if, he asks, with a glancing reference to a conceit formulated by René Descartes, 'a demon crept after you one day or night in your loneliest solitude and said to you: "This life, as you live it now and have lived it, you will have to live it again and again... every pain and every joy... in the same series and sequence. Would you throw yourself down and gnash your teeth... or would you answer... never did I hear anything more divine."

The idea of being able to affirm one's life over and over again is effectively, in *The Gay Science*, an aesthetic judgement that confers value. It is a command to 'become who we are'. It seems to be intended to provide us with the aesthetic stimulus to construct our lives in such a way that they are worth repeating. It can also be read as an existential test that will determine whether life is meaningful.

In the version that appears in his notebooks and subsequently in the posthumous book *The Will to Power*, more problematically, he presented the doctrine as a genuine scientific phenomenon. This transforms it into a cosmological theory that purports to offer an account of the nature of time.

In each form the doctrine is essentially an attempt to provide the meaning of life in life itself. Through it we learn to love and accept fate. It is the ideal way that we can stand in relation to the world.

Lou, Lou Skip To My Lou

The original version of *The Gay Science* closes with the figure of Zarathustra (the Persian prophet) descending from his isolated mountain to rejoin the world of men. After ten years of enjoyable solitude spent accruing knowledge and admiring the world from a glacial vantage point, he decides that his vast intellect would be wasted if he could not share it with others. Nietzsche too was starting to reach the same conclusions about his own life. In 1882 the shapely figure of a young lady called Lou Salome had made him want 'to learn again to be a human being.'

The extraordinary life of Louise von Salome is more than worthy of the biographies that have been devoted to it. She was born in St Petersburg in 1861. Her father, a Baltic German of Huguenot descent was a general in the Russian military. He moved in aristocratic circles and young Lou was raised in a sumptuous apartment just opposite the Winter Palace. A single girl amidst five brothers, she quickly learned to hold her own among the male sex, something then still seen as unusual. Fiercely intelligent and never lacking in confidence Lou beguiled and bewitched some of 19th century Europe's most outstanding cultural figures. Aside from Nietzsche and Paul Ree, her acquaintances and lovers included the poet Rainer Maria Rilke, the dramatist Gerhard Hauptmann and the writers Arthur Schnitzler and Frank Wedekind (whose *Lulu*, memorably filmed by G W Pabst as *Pandora's Box* with Louise Brooks, was inspired by her). In 1912, when she was already an acclaimed writer, she studied psychoanalysis under Sigmund Freud and for the last twenty-five years of her life she became a leading practitioner in her own right.

When Nietzsche met her she was just twenty-one. She had been studying logic, metaphysics and history at Zurich University but after falling ill she had travelled to Italy with her mother, an emotionally cold Danish-German. In Rome she attended meetings at the home of the idealist feminist Malwida von Meysenburg and it was here that she was introduced to Paul Ree. Ree quickly became enamoured of Lou. The pair would walk, arm in arm, through the streets of the city engaged in fierce philosophical debates. Ree eventually asked Lou to marry him. She turned him down but suggested the idea of an intellectual *ménage-a-trois*, where she, Ree and another would live together in Platonic harmony exchanging ideas rather than bodily fluids. Nietzsche, it was decided, was just the man to complete the triangle. The three met in April 1882. Nietzsche was instantly enraptured and mumbled, 'What stars have sent us orbiting towards each other?' This might seem a line that would look happier in a bad Valentine's card than coming from the mouth of one of the world's greatest thinkers but she was impressed. Although not impressed enough to accept the proposal of marriage that he offered her three days later via Ree. 'The Trinity,' as Salome called it, was still on the cards though and the trio, after posing for a photograph where Ree and Nietzsche are harnessed to a cart while Lou brandishes a whip, began to make plans to live and study together in Vienna.

The bizarre love-less triangle, accompanied by Salome Snr, then took a short tour of Switzerland and Italy. Once again Nietzsche proposed to Lou, only this time in person. She again rejected him. Ree it seems also increased his efforts to gain Salome by bombarding her with letters suggesting she become an honorary member of his family, more a sister than a wife. Though tensions were mounting they pushed on with the idea of cohabitation. It was only when Elisabeth, Nietzsche's sister, got wind of the idea that the plan was finally scuppered. Lou had accompanied Elisabeth to Bayreuth for the first performances of Parsifal. The pair had quarrelled almost instantly and Elisabeth quickly wrote to her mother reporting that beloved Fritz was now cavorting with an immoral woman. Over the next couple of months angry scenes between Lou and Elisabeth, Fritz and Elisabeth and Fritz and Franziska took place. When Nietzsche rejoined Ree and Lou in Leipzig in October, they discussed setting up home in Paris to avoid causing a scandal in Germany. Paul and Lou, however, slipped off without arranging to meet up with him and over the next few weeks it slowly dawned on Nietzsche that he had been abandoned. Bitterly disappointed, feeling sick and emotionally exhausted, he shuffled back to Basel and then on to Genoa. At Christmas he wrote to Franz Overbeck in state of extreme agitation. In the letter he veers from wanting, even in the face of these deep personal disappointments, to affirm 'that all experiences are useful', to suggesting that he might 'press on... in solitude and renunciation, till... the point of no return, and -----', indicating that he was on the brink of suicide. By January he had decided that the former was the wiser option and began channelling his anger into art. *Thus Spoke Zarathustra*, he later claimed, was a work that could only be understood by those who had known real pain and disappointment and Nietzsche at the time had more than enough of both.

Oh Superman

'The detail seems to contain an incredible amount of personal experience and the suffering which is intelligible only to me- there are some pages which seemed to drip blood.'

Letter to Peter Gast August 1883

Thus Spoke Zarathustra is one of, if not the most personal of Nietzsche's books. Perhaps this is the reason it is written in verse in an array of differing voices, allowing him to hide behind a series of masks. He described the book's style 'as a dance, a play of symmetries of every kind, and an overleaping mockery of these symmetries.' Adding modestly, 'with this I have brought the German language to a state of perfection.' One can only assume that Nietzsche's idea of perfection was one of excess, for the sheer volume of metaphors, allusions, word play and references is staggering. The heightened, biblical language often makes unnerving and uncomfortable reading especially when in parts it appears driven by bitter misanthropy and rampant misogyny.

The line 'Are you visiting women? Do not forget your whip?' is often quoted but few note that it is actually spoken in the text by a woman and this choice of narrator is significant. It does not excuse some of his choicer rants about women, of which there are quite a few in *Zarathustra*, but it's worth bearing in mind that whilst writing it, Nietzsche was battling to overcome the humiliation of a failed love affair, worsening health, the fear of impeding madness and the feeling that he was once more utterly alone.

Z Is For Zarathustra

'Before Christ Zarathustra emphasised Truth and Righteousness and led people to the right path of life.'

Voltaire

Zarathustra, as we have seen, first appears at the end of *The Gay Science* and the image of him descending from his mountain to rejoin the world of men is repeated in the beginning of *Thus Spoke Zarathustra*. Zarathustra or Zoroaster in Greek, was a Persian prophet who was believed in Hellenic times to have been the first true philosopher before Socrates. Given Nietzsche's adoration/hatred of Socrates and Plato his choice is far from arbitrary. However it would be a mistake to assume that he has returned to the anti-Socratic position that formed the basis for *The Birth of Tragedy*. *Thus Spoke Zarathustra*, for all its flaws, crystallises the ideas he had developed in *Human, All Too Human* and *The Gay Science*, and often in the most profound way.

Zoroaster's dates and even existence are matter of much speculation but he is traditionally believed to have lived, if at all, before Moses, Buddha or Confucius, making him one of the first prophets of any major religion. The beliefs of early Aryan, Persian people were extremely superstitious and Zoroaster, after experiencing seven revelations, is reputed to have set out to combat superstition. His task was not easy and, after ten years of fruitlessly preaching his doctrine of the seven wills, he departed for distant lands. When he returned from the wilderness he found the world more willing to accept his views and while he is reputed to have died at the age of 77 (the mystical number of 7 repeated once again) Zoroastrianism flourished. By 500 BC it was established as the state religion of the Persian Empire. It is usually and presently practised as a dualistic religion. However there are other interpretations. A strand of Zoroastrianism posits that good and evil are not inherently connected to two gods or creators (God/Devil) but essential qualities that exist within all creatures and one of its key tenets is that there is no fear of evil because man has the faculties to discern right and wrong.

Thus Spoke Zarathustra

Nietzsche's Zarathustra appears as an anti-Christ seer. Like the Persian prophet his main aim is to make us cast off superstition i.e. religion, science and metaphysical speculation. At the beginning of the book he begins by expounding his vision of the *Übermensch* or superman to a crowd gathered for a circus. For all of the bluster concerning the Superman it actually features very little elsewhere in the work. His descriptions of quite whom or what is meant to embody the *Übermensch* are opaque to say the least. Sentences like, 'Behold I am the prophet of lightning and a heavy drop from the clouds: but this lightning is called superman' are not exactly illuminating. Nietzsche wants to differentiate the Superman from what he calls the Ultimate Men, those who believe that happiness lies in personal comfort and material goods. They want an easy life and blindly go along with the herd, accepting its sham morality and dogma. The supermen are those who reject this and construct their own characters, beliefs and values. Whether Nietzsche believes this is an evolutionary state or a mental attitude is open to debate.

Zarathustra, he says 'has seen many lands and many peoples' and has discovered 'that what was called evil in one place was in another decked with purple.' Here he seems to be proposing a form of relativism where morality is connection to custom but in the next paragraph he introduces what could be construed as a universal and even metaphysical concept. 'A table of values hangs over every people…. behold, it is the voice of its will to power.' The will to power is a continuation of the critique of Christian morality that began in *Human, All Too Human* but here it is effectively presented as the force that drives all value systems. 'Where I found a living creature' he says 'there I found will to power; and even in the will of the servant I found the will to be master.'

Unlike the Schopenhauerian will, to which it bears more than a passing resemblance, Nietzschean will to power is a striving of the self. All creatures want more power but in man this apparently Darwinian urge to dominate others extends to the self. Nietzsche is all too aware of the subtle delineations in what and how power manifests itself and argues that the weak turned the lust for power on themselves and learned to obey self-imposed rules for an easier existence. They gave up their humanity to become a people. Social constraints are therefore not just a matter of custom but also arise from the need to assert power. Man has the ability to achieve self-mastery and as the Übermensch is for Nietzsche a non-metaphysical transcendent being, it symbolises the ultimate stage in human development. The Übermensch is able to reject the false values that have arisen from sublimated power drives, recognising (somewhat paradoxically) that all claims to truth are derived from the battle between conflicting wills to power and that therefore they must create themselves or, as Nietzsche puts it, 'become… who they are.' They, as the literal translation suggests, overcome man. The Übermensch who has created himself is there able to affirm the whole of life again and again because they accept every struggle as an essential part of existence.

It is hard not to read much of *Thus Spoke Zarathustra* as directly autobiographical. His championing of solitude, the need to endure cold, discomfort and rejection all have the whiff of a man who is indeed cold, uncomfortable and rejected. Which was of course exactly what he was.

The transformation of the Superman from one who overcomes man into one who stomps his fellow man into the ground with a jackboot is one of the world's greatest tragedies and a remarkable exercise in selective reading. Unfortunately for Nietzsche and for humanity as a whole such an interpretation had a helping hand from his own sister.

'My Sister And I'

Relations between Fritz and Lama following the Ree/Salome affair were far from cordial. In the summer of 1883 Nietzsche wrote that he was possessed by 'a real hatred' of his sister. The situation was not improved when he learned that she had become engaged to Dr. Bernhard Förster, a notorious anti-Semite. Förster was a former schoolteacher and a founding member of the German People's Party - a political organisation with a rigid idea of who were German people and who weren't. Elisabeth had first met Förster in 1882 and he had accompanied her to that year's Bayreuth festival. The vegetarian Förster, who advocated the removal of all Jews from Prussia, no doubt cut quite a dash among the rest of the toadying proto-fascists at the festival. During the 1870s he had been one of the 'German Seven', a vociferous bunch of anti-Semites who had plagued the nation with pamphlets calling for the exclusions of Jews from positions of influence. In 1880 he'd had to resign from his teaching position after being involved in a racially motivated punch-up on a tram. Jobless but unbowed he drew up a petition to Bismarck, calling for the limitation of Jewish immigrants. Bismarck sensibly chose to ignore it. Unable to drum up enough interest in a Jew-free Germany, he set upon the idea of forming a New Germany on soil uncorrupted by Jewry. Land in Paraguay was duly acquired.

Nietzsche was flabbergasted that his sister could have fallen among the anti-Semites so easily. He referred to her as a 'silly anti-Semitic goose' and could only poke fun of Förster's plans. In a letter to his mother he noted that the 'vegetarian diet, which Dr. Förster requires, makes... (the Germans) more susceptible to gloom. The 'meat-eating' English - now that was a race which knew best how to found colonies. Phlegm and roast beef - that was till now the recipe for such an undertaking.'

Elisabeth married Förster on the 22nd of May 1885, Wagner's birthday. Nietzsche did not attend and wrote 'forgive me for not coming to your wedding - such a "sick" philosopher would be a bad person to give the bride away!' In fact, as his letter to Franz Overbeck a few months later shows, he found the whole idea of meeting his brother-in-law utterly repugnant. 'There are', he felt, 'good reasons for not trusting the anti-Semites any further than one can see them.' When he did meet Förster in October of that year he found him not 'unpleasant'. Hardly a ringing endorsement. The Försters left for South America in 1886 and Nietzsche was freed from making small talk with his brother-in-law for the foreseeable future. As it was he never saw him again. The colony proved to be a disaster and three years later Förster took a pistol and blew his brains out to avoid bankruptcy and prosecution. In letters home Elisabeth quaintly described his death as the result of a 'nervous attack.'

Beyond Good And Evil

In keeping with his own maxim: 'He who has to be a creator always has to destroy.' Nietzsche saw *Beyond Good and Evil* as the first stage in a fundamental assault on existing values. His target this time was the very notion of truth itself. 'What really is it in us that wants truth?' he asks. 'Granted that we want truth: why not rather untruth? And uncertainty? Even ignorance?' Philosophers, he contends, have always assumed that truth was valuable without bothering to consider whether it actually was or not. Worse than that they always claimed to reach their discoveries by pure cold, reason. Nothing, he argues, could be further from the (ultimately unknowable) truth. Every great philosophy is actually 'a confession on the part of its author... a kind of involuntary and unconscious memoir.' They have all consistently failed to realise that when they attempted to define morality, they were already carrying a sack-load of personal prejudices and cultural assumptions. For Nietzsche the will to truth is inextricably bound to the will to power. All claims to truth are therefore psychologically produced fictions that serve the deepest desires of whoever is proposing them. So far, so proto-Freudian. If the countless tomes and treatises of the world's thinkers are culturally determined then what about the very language in which they are written? Here Nietzsche offers his most devastating blow. Since philosophical systems are delivered in a language they must be subject to the rules and history of that language. Even the statement 'I think', which Rene Descartes thought so immune from doubt, is a product of grammar. As Nietzsche gleefully points out, 'Whence do I take the concept thinking? What gives me the right to speak of an 'I', and even of an 'I' as cause, and finally of an 'I' as cause of thought.' 'A thought comes when 'it' wants to, not when 'I' want; so… it is a falsification of the facts to say the subject 'I' is the condition of the predicate 'think'.' It is only because western language has developed with a penchant for subjects and verbs that we have been tempted to posit the idea of an inner self. He goes on to add that 'philosophers within the domain of the Ural-Altaic languages (in which the concept of the subject is least developed)… look into the world differently.' Quite how differently, and in what way, he doesn't bother to say but I think we can possibly accept his point. Like Wittgenstein who stated some years later that if lions could talk we wouldn't be able to understand them, Nietzsche is claiming that our form of life is fundamental both to how languages develop and, in turn, how we come to analyse the world. Given this the central tenet of Descartes' philosophy is not a profound statement of truth but a kink in the language that just exposes the predilections of a 17th century French mathematician.

If this is 'true' what are philosophers supposed to do? As the book is subtitled ' A Prelude to a Philosophy of the Future', Nietzsche offers his view on what the new philosophers must do. They will be 'commanders and law-givers: they say "Thus it shall be!", it is they who determine the Wherefore and Whither of mankind...they search for the future with creative hand. Their "knowing" is creating… their will to truth is - will to power.' The new philosophers are those who are brave enough and bright enough to accept the harsh 'truth' that we must live without truth and go on to create and affirm their existences. The question of the value of truth for Nietzsche is intrinsically connected to the question of moral values because moral values characteristically seek to establish themselves as truths. Returning once more to an old hobby-horse he argues that Western culture has effectively been hijacked since the time of the Greeks. In Ancient Greece 'designations of moral value were first applied to human beings and only later and derivatively to actions.' What he calls the master morality or noble type of man 'feels himself to be the determiner of values, he does not need to be approved of, he creates values.' Nietzsche contrasts the sentiments of these noble thinkers with what he feels is the prevailing decadent, herd mentality of his own age. Slave morality, as he names it is, arose from those who were suspicious of the virtues of the powerful with the result that a sickly mediocre culture developed that relied on transcendent values to make life worth living. In Nietzsche's view the herd values of timidity and humility are against nature because living creatures want to 'vent their strengths - life as such is will to power.'

As even the most casual reader must have noticed by now, Nietzsche's views are unrepentantly elitist. Yet it is doubtful that he really believed such a new breed of thinkers was possible or perhaps even welcome. He asks: Are there such philosophers today? Have there been such philosophers? Must there not be such philosophers? What he really wants is more honesty about what exactly is going on when people embark on philosophising. He playfully ends the book with a comment on his own philosophy: 'Alas... my written and painted thoughts! Not long ago you were still so-many-coloured, young and malicious, so full of thorns and hidden spices you made me laugh and sneeze. - and now? You have already taken off your novelty and some of you I fear are on the brink of becoming truths: so pathetically righteous, so boring!'

Because reality, for Nietzsche is never fixed and permanent, philosophy must always be a work of creative play. It is the work of an imaginative not logical mind and can never aspire to express truth. As such, even his own work is subject to interpretation, doubt and even dismissal.

The Gene Genie

The Genealogy of Morals is a companion or sequel to *Beyond Good and Evil*. Subtitled 'A Polemic', it is a whole book on a theme that in his last had only been allotted a chapter. Organised into three, actually quite cogent sections, *The Genealogy of Morals* is a sustained attempt to explain, cajole or force us to believe, how the concepts of good and evil evolved. This largely consists of him contrasting how 'good' became established in societies of master and slave moralities. Language, Nietzsche claims, developed because the dominant relished their power as name givers. 'By saying 'this is such and such', they put their seal on each thing and event with a sound and, in the process, take possession of it.' The idea of an upper or aristocratic class controlling language is not the stuff of ancient history. Orlando Figes' study of the Russian Revolution, *A People's Tragedy* relates how, at the beginning of the twentieth century, Russian peasants with names whose etymological roots stemmed from terms like 'ugly' and 'smelly' would still have to write to the Tsar for a special dispensation to change them. If Nietzsche is (as always) keen to promote the cause of an antique elite it is worth noting that, however biased his description of how language formed is, in a country only a few hundred miles from where he was raised, many ordinary people were still unable to choose their own names.

Less easy to accept are some of Nietzsche's more dubious claims about whom the noble or master races were. The Gaelic word 'Fin', as in Fin-Gal the Irish mythological hero, he claims 'characterised the nobility, which ultimately meant the good, the noble, the pure, but originally the blond-headed, in contrast to the swarthy, dark-haired original inhabitants.' He then backs this up with one of his most misunderstood statements. 'There is no mistaking the predator beneath the surface of all these noble races, the magnificent blond beast roaming lecherously in search of booty and victory.' However, Nietzsche then adds that 'Roman, Arab, German, Japanese nobility, Homeric heroes, Scandinavian Vikings... all share the same need.' As at least three or even four of these groups are not usually purchasers of camomile shampoo, the blond beast is clearly not intended to be a symbol of white power. It is usually interpreted as a lion, representing the ruthlessness of aristocratic morality. If this seems like letting Nietzsche off the hook too easily it also worth noting that when he formulates his theory of *ressentiment*, the idea that justice is the weak's attempt to enact revenge on those more imaginative and powerful than themselves, he argues that this tendency 'blooms most beautifully among anti-Semites.' Hardly a sign that Nietzsche saw himself as an advocate of Teutonic supremacy.

His point is that noble human beings of any colour or creed are naturally predatory. Over time though the victims or slaves have managed to wreak their revenge by equating the aristocratic contempt for safety and moderation with evil. The Judaeo-Christian obsession with denigrating the body and 'repressing' desires he feels has made man into a sickly and mediocre creature. In a section that pre-empts both Freud and Jung he speaks of the mind's ability to actively forget our natural urges. With this forgetfulness we turned our cruelty in upon ourselves and came to posit the idea of conscience and a soul. Nietzsche contends it is time for man to realise how ill s/he is.

4. Mad? - The Final Years

1888, the last sane year of Nietzsche's life (if occasionally only tenuously so), was staggeringly productive. He worked on five books and amended some poems dating from the Zarathustra period. The publication of *The Genealogy of Morals* the previous autumn had brought Nietzsche something he had secretly craved all along, critical acclaim. Georg Brandes, a Danish literary critic and historian who had written an influential study of Kierkegaard, wrote to him praising his 'aristocratic radicalism' and announced that he was going to begin lecturing on his work. Nietzsche was overjoyed and furnished him with copies of his earlier books and a self-aggrandising curriculum vitae that shows quite how unstable his mental condition was. In it he claims to be descended from Polish nobility, 'versed in the use of two weapons: sabre and cannon- and, perhaps, one other… ', to share the same pulse rate as Napoleon and to be by instinct a 'courageous, even military' animal. Nietzsche seemed to have forgotten his distinctly ineffectual spells in the army but by now illness had shorn him of his modesty.

Spaghetti Hoops

In the spring Nietzsche moved to Turin, a city he referred to as a 'princely residence', and finished writing *The Case of Wagner*, a short, garbled polemic against his old mentor. He describes the composer as 'just one' of his 'sicknesses' and equates the composer, who by that time had been dead for five years, with Germany's and the modern world's cultural malaise. Wagner for Nietzsche is a decadent and as such is responsible for peddling nihilism - a cardinal sin in his joyful and life affirming anti-church. 'Have you ever noticed', he

54

says at one point, 'that Wagner's heroines never have children?' To breed would be to propagate life, something far too gruesome for Wagner, the inheritor of Schopenhauer's pessimism, to contemplate. Much of the book, and it is a very slim one, is spent contrasting the gloominess of Wagner's music with the gay spirit of Bizet. Written at the time when the Meister was regarded almost as a god in his native land, few would have taken his view that Bizet was a healthier composer seriously. Many of his former friends and colleagues regarded the book as opportunistic and a sign that the philosopher had a severe attack of sour grapes. Nietzsche himself must have realised this because his final work *Nietzsche contra Wagner*, completed just before his collapse, was an anthology of passages from his earlier writings intended to show that his opinions on Wagner were established some years before the composer's death.

Sing A Song At Twilight

Wagner was clearly playing on Nietzsche's mind when he came to write his next book. Although he appears only infrequently in it he did provide the inspiration for its title. *Twilight of the Idols*, is a pun on Wagner's *Götterdämerung*, Twilight of the Gods. *Twilight of the Idols*, subtitled 'How To Philosophize With A Hammer', is not one of Nietzsche's most subtle books. Described as 'a 'grand declaration of war' by its author, its tone is strident at the very least. It begins by returning to a critique of Socrates he had first outlined in *The Birth of Tragedy*. The ancient Athenian and his disciple Plato are castigated, once more, for destroying Greek culture. Socrates was a sick and decadent philosopher who wanted to die. He had rejected this world, preferring to believe in an 'ideal world' behind it and in doing so had condemned philosophy to spend several thousand years ploughing the same furrow. The equation of reason with virtue and happiness led to the denial of life and with it the whole sorry mess of Christianity and moral hypocrisy. Nietzsche restates here his belief that the Church 'corrupted the human being, it weakened him – but claimed to have "improved" him.' What had previously been regard as strong and happy impulses for life were now sins and the sinners were crippled by ill-will towards themselves. He argues, like Marx, that religion was the great European narcotic. In his own country however, this had been supplemented by beer, yet another sign for Nietzsche that German culture is characterised by degeneracy and sluggishness. (Nietzsche's own drunken student days were obviously a distant memory by now as illness prevented him from drinking alcohol in anything but minimal quantities.) He lambasts the mediocrity of Germany, claiming that Deutschland, Deutschland Über Alles marked the 'end of German philosophy.' Goethe is seen as the last truly great German because, inspired by Napoleon, he 'conceived of a strong highly cultured human being... who is strong enough for freedom. A man to whom nothing is forbidden, except... weakness, whether that weakness be called vice or virtue. A spirit thus emancipated stands in the midst of the universe with a trusting fatalism.' Nietzsche sees this spirit as Dionysian and argues that the Hellenic instinct was always a 'will to life'. 'It was only Christianity, with *ressentiment* against life, which made sexuality something impure.' Throwing 'filth on the beginning, on the prerequisite of life.' He concludes by again harking back to his first book claiming that it was 'the first revaluation of all values' and that he, the teacher of the eternal recurrence, has again returned to his starting point.

The Anti-Christian

Curiously, given his claim in *Twilight of the Idols,* that *The Birth of Tragedy* was the first revaluation of all values, *The Anti-Christ* or Anti-Christian, is described by Nietzsche in *Ecce Homo* as the 'first book of the Revaluation of all Values'. At this point he still planned to write possibly four books presenting a definitive version of his philosophy under that title. He had already abandoned a series of notes provisionally called *The Will to Power* and it appears he was anxious to begin work, no doubt spurred on by the interest of Brandes, on what he hoped would be his greatest achievement. Unfortunately insanity called time on that and, as in *Twilight of the Idols*, much of what appears in *The Anti-Christ* is not so much substantially new philosophical opinions as reiterations and more recklessly expressed versions of old ones. 'What is good?' he asks. 'All that heightens the feeling of power, the will to power, power itself in man', he replies. 'What is bad?' 'All that proceeds from weakness', is the answer. What is responsible for the modern world's ills? Christianity which 'has made an ideal out of opposition to the preservative instincts of strong life.' Nietzsche doesn't so much repeat the arguments he made in *Beyond Good and Evil* and *The Genealogy of Morals* as assume they are already established. The result is that *The Anti-Christ* is his most bombastic, if ill-substantiated, attack on the Christian religion.

According to Nietzsche, central to the insidious aims of the Judaeo-Christian God-botherers has been the notion of pity. 'We are', he maintains, 'deprived of strength when we feel pity.' Pity multiplies suffering because it allows us to suffer along with those for whom we feel pity. This depresses us but in turn also allows those whom nature, as he delicately puts, has deemed 'ripe for destruction' to feed off our strength. The end result is that the strong are weakened and the weak survive.

All this began when the formerly noble ancient Jews found themselves oppressed by Rome during the occupation of Palestine. Deprived of power, they transformed their proud warrior-god into a god of the weak and oppressed in order to reflect and make a virtue of their own condition. Christianity therefore inherited a sick and ailing deity to 'whom the rapturous ardours of victory and destruction were unknown.' He offers a few words of praise for Buddhism. It might also, he believes, be a nihilistic religion but at least it doesn't carry any moral baggage. The Buddhist is primarily concerned with avoiding suffering and is not concerned with making moral judgements about others. They live passively and demand 'no struggle against those who think differently.' 'In the teaching of Buddhism egoism becomes a duty... the "how can *you* be rid of suffering" regulates the spiritual diet.' Through moderation and by avoiding any excitement the Buddhist actually achieves his or her aims and manages to live a contented life on earth. Conversely Christian ascetic lifestyle demands the removal of sin with the end result that the disciple is left in a state of turmoil, constantly yearning for forgiveness.

Nietzsche having constructed this point goes on to argue that the historical figure of Jesus was actually far closer to Buddhism. Jesus was not the redeemer of mankind but offered a way to live. Like Buddhists he did not resist his accusers. He 'entreats, he suffers, he loves with those, *in* those who are doing evil to him.' It was only after his death that his followers, bitter from his loss, wanted vengeance. They failed to realise that, like him, they should have forgiven his enemies and instead sought to exact their revenge on the Jewish hierarchy by claiming he was the Messiah. If this was true how could God have allowed him to die? They hit on the idea that 'God gave his Son for the forgiveness of sins, as a sacrifice… the sacrifice of the innocent man for the sins of the guilty!' From then on arose 'the doctrine of a judgement and a Second Coming.' So what should have been 'an actual and not merely promised happiness on earth' was dashed and in its place the early church and particularly Paul, as Nietzsche stresses, constructed a life-denying religion.

Christianity was so potent that even philosophy was infected with the urge to reject the body and seek solace in metaphysical constructions. Nietzsche, on this occasion passes up the opportunity to denounce Plato and goes on to point the finger of blame closer to home. The Germans - from Luther to Kant and beyond - had promoted this kind of decadent reasoning. Just to hammer the point home he adds that 'if we never get rid of Christianity, the Germans will be to blame.' If one was left in any doubt to his feelings about the religion of his forefathers he concludes the book by utterly condemning it. Christianity is for Nietzsche 'the one great curse, the one great instinct for revenge for which no expedient is sufficiently poisonous, secret, subterranean, petty… the one immortal blemish of mankind.'

The Anti-Christ is historically inaccurate, relies on a covert acceptance of his concept of the will to power and at times, like *The Case of Wagner*, reads more like a letter from a spurned lover than a serious attempt at a revaluation of all values. Yet despite all this there is something psychologically convincing about its searing indictments of the aims and motives of the church. One is left in no doubt as to Nietzsche's unwavering, if elitist, belief in the potential for human life.

The Ego Has Landed

On the 15th October 1888, Nietzsche celebrated his forty-fourth birthday in Turin. He received just one letter, from the ever-loyal Peter Gast, and marked the occasion by beginning work on *Ecce Homo*, his distinctly strange autobiography. Two weeks later he described it to Gast as a work that 'concerns, with great audacity myself and my writings.' Modesty had rarely troubled Nietzsche in his, relatively, sane life but now, gripped by euphoria, he felt few qualms about proclaiming his genius. His comments on Turin in the same letter give some indication of the extent to which he was no longer willing or able to make rational judgements about himself or his surroundings. 'My room' he says, is in the 'best position in the centre, sunshine from early morning until afternoon, view on the Palazzo Carignano, the Piazza Carlo Alberto and across and away to the green mountains.' In fact Turin has an average of 107 rainy days a year and Nietzsche's room, which had a limited view of the Piazza Carlo Alberto, was in a pension only yards from the railway station and dwarfed by two gigantic, gloomy buildings.

Ecce Homo, subtitled 'How One Becomes What One Is', takes its main title - literally 'Behold the Man'- from Pilate's words about Christ in St John's Gospel. If the title is provocative what follows is little short of a Mexican wave of egotism. With chapter headings such as 'Why I Write Such Good Books', 'Why I am So Clever' and 'Why I am Destiny', Nietzsche maps whole new territories in self-belief. Once again he is simply making overt what is normally left covert. Even the most modest autobiographies are always acts of narcissism; Nietzsche just cranks the thing up to eleven and mocks the entire genre. It is a mischievous, impish book but one full of chillingly accurate pronouncements. He says of his own fate that, 'One day there will be associated with my name the recollection of something frightful- of a crisis like no other before on earth… I am not a man, I am dynamite.' Few philosophers have ever predicted their legacy so correctly.

Like *Thus Spoke Zarathustra*, which here he coyly describes as the 'greatest gift' mankind has ever been given, much of *Ecce Homo* extols the virtues of Nietzsche's own austere lifestyle. In fact some of it reads like a self-help book - a kind of Heal Your Life the Nietzsche way. Though he claims to have put away a fair share of booze as a youth, alcohol should be avoided. 'Water suffices' and he prefers 'places where there is an opportunity to drink from flowing fountains.' 'A big meal', we learn, is 'easier to digest than one too small.' There should be 'no eating between meals' and no coffee because it makes people 'gloomy'. Ideally we should start the day with 'a cup of oil-free cocoa' and then follow that with some strong tea. 'Sit as little as possible' and 'credit no thought not born in the open air.' Prejudices apparently all 'come from the intestines.' Nietzsche, who announces at the beginning of the book he is a 'pure-blooded Polish nobleman', maintains that 'the German climate alone is enough to discourage strong and heroic intestines.' Genius, Fritz argues from his sunny Turin residence, 'is conditioned by dry air.' Only in the climes of Paris, Florence and Jerusalem can a rapid metabolism develop. Nietzsche declares he was lucky. If he hadn't been ill he too might have languished in Germany and become, like a friend of his, 'a narrow, withdrawn, grumpy specialist.' Instead illness brought him reason. He was able to see how sick and vengeful instincts had corrupted philosophy and spread the pernicious Christian doctrine. When he was healthy he fell victim to pessimism - to Schopenhauer and Wagner. He too was a decadent but in combating his sickness he made his will to health and to life his philosophy and became their antithesis. He was able to become what he is by avoiding grand imperatives. By accepting the condition of his life, employing his ill chances to his own advantage because he understood that 'what does not kill him makes him stronger', he has been able to affirm life. It is for this reason he is so interested in discussing the influence of climate, nutriment, place and recreation. It is precisely because it is ignored by other thinkers who, once again, wish to deny life in favour of metaphysical chimeras. 'Contempt', he adds, 'has been taught for the little things, which is to say for the fundamental affairs of life.'

He is therefore not surprised he has remained unread in his native Germany, a land still wedded to the stodgy idealism of Kant and Hegel. Wagner's downfall, he notes, was to condescend to the Germans; he became a *reichdeutsch*. Nietzsche on the other hand is, or so he rather disingenuously claims, 'utterly incurious about discussions' of his books in the German press. He doesn't need to be as he says he has 'readers everywhere else… in Vienna, in St Petersburg, in Stockholm, in Paris' and, even more surprisingly, in New York. More astonishing yet is his belief that, in Turin, 'faces grow more cheerful and benevolent' at the sight of him and that the old market-women take the greatest pains to select 'the sweetest of their grapes' for him. While it is not impossible that Nietzsche was a valued customer it seems unlikely that the people of Turin would really have been heartened by the appearance of a virtually blind Prussian who, in his own words, looked like a mountain sheep. However, a man willing to state that he reinvented the German language, that his instincts were infallible and that either Julius Caesar or Alexander could realistically be seen as his father, is, at this point in his life, no longer a reliable witness.

Whilst most of the book is devoted to setting out his former achievements the final part, Why I Am Destiny, looks to the future. Having cleansed the world of the placebo of Christianity he fears that he 'shall be one day pronounced holy.' His 'truth is dreadful: for hitherto the lie has been called truth' and when 'truth steps into battle with the lie of millennia we shall have convulsions'. In a phrase that proved more reliable than anything in Nostradamus he predicts that ' there will be wars such as there have never yet been on earth.' Nietzsche calls himself the first immoralist, the most terrible human being because he has exposed the lies that have been crippling humanity. Keeping true to his Dionysian nature, he revels in their destruction. Some will call his superman a devil because they would be frightened of his true goodness but the unmasking of Christian morality calls for the shattering of all values. His Zarathustra, whom, confusingly, in this section he presents as both a character and as an embodiment of himself, is the only one, at the present, capable of bearing this awful truth. Whether Nietzsche himself really could was quite another matter.

Philosopher And Philip

With *Ecce Homo* completed, Nietzsche began assembling *Nietzsche Contra Wagner*, a compendium of his various earlier writings on the composer that he hoped would settle what he called 'the Wagner questions' once and for all. It is clear from the more extravagant pronouncements in *Ecce Homo* and from his correspondence that, in the autumn of 1888, Nietzsche's mental health took a sharp turn for the worse. By December his tone abruptly shifts from what at best could be described as exuberant to maniacal. A letter to Carl Fuchs on 18th December begins with a breezy declaration of rude health before announcing that, as the old God has abdicated, he, Nietzsche, will rule the world from now on. Days later Franz Overbeck was informed that he was working on a memorandum to form an anti-German league and that he would not rest until 'the young emperor and all his appurtenances' were in his hands. Overbeck replied anxiously, inquiring after Nietzsche's health. The philosopher's reply, dated the 31st, was surprisingly calm. He explained he had written it in 'a bad light' and 'no longer knew what' he was writing. On the same day, however, in a letter to Peter Gast he rambled on about the Rubicon and confessed to no longer knowing his address, whilst, in one to the dramatist August Strindberg, Nietzsche stated that he had 'ordered a convocation of princes in Rome' and that he meant 'to have the young emperor shot.' It was signed 'Nietzsche Caesar'.

The date of Nietzsche's dramatic collapse is normally given as the 3rd of January 1889. Though accounts vary there is no reason to doubt that the event usually associated with his breakdown did occur. Whether he was already unhinged at that point or only afterwards is a bone of contention. What is in no doubt is that from the 4th of January onwards Nietzsche could no longer be regarded in any common definition as sane. As Nietzsche was leaving his house he saw on the Piazza Carlo Alberto, where the horse-drawn cabs were parked, a tired old horse being beaten by a brutal cabman. He rushed forward and flung his arms around the animal, burst into tears and then collapsed. His landlord Davide Fino, attracted by a small crowd that had gather around his tenant, carried him back to his room. When he awoke he was clearly disturbed and began singing, shouting, thumping at the piano and generally acting in a frenzied manner. (Tellingly, his sister Elisabeth's version of his collapse does differ from the more famous story. In her account he simply falls off a high pavement. This may suggest she was all too aware of the real story but decided that an actual, and indeed metaphorical, fall would appear more dignified.) When Nietzsche had calmed down he wrote a series of notes to the King of Italy, the royal house at Baden and the Vatican Secretary of State and told Fino that he was going to Rome to meet the pope and the princes of Europe. Letters to Gast, Overbeck and Burckhardt respectively declared that the world was transformed and all the heavens were rejoicing, that he was 'just having all anti-Semites shot' and that he 'would much rather be a Basel professor than God.' They were signed either The Crucified or Dionysus. Cosima Wagner received a declaration of love, possibly long latent. Overbeck, after showing the letters he had received to the head physician at Basel's insane asylum, travelled to Turin to discover what had happened to Nietzsche.

He arrived just in time; the landlord, who had shown considerable tolerance, was in the process of fetching the police with the intention of having Nietzsche taken to a private insane asylum. Overbeck found his friend crouched over the proofs of *Nietzsche Contra Wagner*, 'looking horribly worn out.' Nietzsche recognised him and violently embraced him, broke into tears and then lay down on his sofa, twitching and quivering. After a few sips of bromide water he became calm again but was convinced that a huge reception was awaiting him. Overbeck's own letters detailing his first impressions, note that, although he seemed lucid when dealing with other people, he had no idea about himself, genuinely believing he was the successor of God and that his job was to be the clown for all eternities. He decided to transport his friend back to Basel and commit him to the care of the local asylum. Getting Nietzsche on the train to take him there proved difficult. Having coaxed him from his bed and got him to the station by convincing him that a pageant was being held in his honour in Basel, the party had to wait an hour for a train. Nietzsche grew restless; he wanted to address the crowds whom he believed had gathered to see him off. Luckily an orderly Overbeck had hired to assist him managed to persuade Nietzsche that he was too important not to travel incognito and that he must do his utmost to avoid being recognised, a plan with which the patient readily concurred. In Basel he was admitted to Professor Wille's nerve clinic. Nietzsche recognised Wille from his time at the university but did not grasp that he had left or ever been in Turin. He was equally unaware that he was a patient and apologised to the staff about the poor weather, offering to prepare them some better weather for the following day.

Nietzsche's mother was sent for and arrived in Basel on the 14th of January. Nietzsche surprised everyone by not only recognising her but also by embarking on a cogent discussion of family matters. All was progressing smoothly until he suddenly started bellowing that he was the tyrant of Turin and the interview had to be terminated. Franziska wanted to take her son home and care for him there but Wille and Overbeck felt this was unwise, given the unpredictability of Nietzsche's condition. Eventually a compromise was reached. Nietzsche would be transferred to the clinic at Jena, where his mother could visit him but he would receive the medical attention he needed.

Another fraught train journey ensued. After initially being pacified with ham sandwiches and cherries Nietzsche began shouting at his mother and threw his gloves out of the train window, with the result that Franziska had to travel in a separate carriage from Frankfurt onwards. At Jena he was admitted to the psychiatric clinic and underwent an extensive three-day period of assessment and examination at the end of which he was diagnosed with 'a paralytic psychic disorder'. Now he was chattering almost continually, his sleep patterns were extremely erratic - even when heavily sedated - and he could no longer tell who he was, claiming to be Friedrich Wilhelm IV or the Duke of Cumberland if asked. Over the next few months however he became calmer and complained of headaches and pains around his eyes. In January of 1890 Peter Gast visited him and found that, although he was prone to childish antics, he didn't seem, on the surface, as ill as he had been. Gast even wondered if the madness was not feigned, another mask that Nietzsche had chosen to adopt. By May he was considered sufficiently docile to be discharged into his mother's care. They lived briefly in Jena before returning to Naumburg where they settled in the very house that Nietzsche had left as a boy of fourteen when he went to attend Pforta.

The Ugly Sister Returns

At the time of her brother's collapse Elisabeth was still in Paraguay. Life in the colony was not going well and in June 1889 her husband committed suicide rather than face legal proceedings against him. After his death she remained there for a further eighteen months before returning to Germany to raise funds and drum up interest in a hagiography she was planning to write about Förster. When she first returned she took little interest in her brother. Instead she busied herself with her own projects, spending most of her time in Berlin. When articles began appearing discussing Nietzsche's philosophy and his condition, however, she began to take a more active interest, if not in his health, then in his work. Gast, Overbeck and Naumann (Nietzsche's publisher) had spoken to Franziska about what should become of her son's writings and Elisabeth quickly became embroiled in the discussions. She managed to delay the publication of the fourth part of *Thus Spoke Zarathustra* - which at that point had only been privately printed - but did eventually agree that a cheap edition of his works should be produced. She returned to South America in July 1892, assuring Gast that whatever happened to the remaining unpublished material (which at that time still included *The Anti-Christ* and *Ecce Homo*), he would be involved. During the remainder of 1892 Gast, with Franziska's permission, began the task of assembling Nietzsche's notes and papers with the aim of producing a definitive edition of his friend's work, backed with prefaces and commentaries by himself. This project was swiftly derailed by the reappearance of Elisabeth. An article in the *Südamerikanische Kolonial-Nachrichten*, a German newspaper devoted to colonial affairs had accused Förster and Elisabeth of maliciously defrauding other colonists and another piece written by a former colony member, urged the citizens of New Germania to expel Elisabeth if she would not leave voluntarily. Elisabeth didn't wait to be asked and, after deposing of her remaining assets, she returned to Germany. No sooner had she arrived than she dispensed with Gast's services as editor and installed Fritz Koegel in his place. She then set about constructing what she christened the Nietzsche Archive; a ludicrous Wunderkammer of her brother's manuscripts, waste paper and ephemera. For the time being this had a rather startling living exhibit - the philosopher himself.

Nietzsche's guardian and the lawful owner of his copyrights was his mother but in 1895 Elisabeth managed to persuade Franziska to sign the rights over to her. By this time the royalties from Nietzsche's publications had become quite substantial. Some fourteen thousand marks were paid into the Nietzsche account at the end of 1894, of which Elisabeth took over five thousand. Having secured control of all future incomes Frau Förster, or Frau Förster-Nietzsche as she was now calling herself, moved to Weimar, taking the archive but not her brother with her. Nietzsche continued to be cared for by his mother and the family servant Alwine in Naumburg. The philosopher really had now reached a state that could be described as beyond good and evil. He barely recognised old friends, spoke infrequently and, when not actually asleep, gazed out at the world in an almost comatose state. The spring of 1897 was unusually cool and damp and, in April, Franziska contracted influenza and died. She was seventy-one and had spent the last seven years dutifully caring for her son.

Nietzsche, whose final work was resolutely contra Wagner, found himself installed in Weimar, the site of his old mentor's Teutonic dreamscape. Elisabeth dressed him in the white robes of a Brahmin and Rudolf Steiner, who was, at the time, closely involved with the archive, is quoted as saying that he gave the impression of being a man who could not die. Possibly because, to all intents and purposes, he was already dead. Even The Anti-Christ proved to be Human, All Too Human and after suffering a stroke in 1899 his condition worsened. On 20th August 1900 he went down with a cold, developed a fierce temperature and died just four days later. He was fifty-five years old. Elisabeth arranged a full Lutheran funeral for the fierce critic of Christianity and even Gast, who gave the funeral oration, proclaimed, 'Holy be thy name to all future generations.'

'I have a terrible fear that one day I shall be pronounced holy... '

Ecce Homo

5. It's What Happens To You When You Are Dead That You Have To Worry About

In the years immediately following his death Nietzsche achieved the recognition he had so desperately craved and Elisabeth provided his audience with a stream of new publications. Between 1901 and 1913 a nineteen volume edition of Nietzsche's works appeared. It included assorted pieces of what is normally called the Nachlas, various bits of unpublished writings, doodles and jottings. The most famous volume of these appeared in 1901 under the title *The Will to Power*. Quite how these writings should be viewed still divides scholars. At the time of his breakdown even his close friends Peter Gast and Franz Overbeck were uncertain about what to do with his unpublished work. Both felt uneasy about *Ecce Homo*, which wasn't published until 1908, but they realised its value and assumed it should be published eventually. (Nietzsche himself had got as far as returning a second draft of the book to his publisher weeks before his collapse.) Though Nietzsche had toyed with and even begun work on a book called *The Will to Power* in 1887, he had abandoned the project in favour of producing the Revaluation of All Values, the first part of which was *The Anti-Christ*. Although there is much in *The Will to Power* that is as extraordinary as any of his published works (Heidegger even argued it was the most complete version of his philosophy) perhaps one should be sceptical of a volume compiled by Elisabeth which includes papers that Nietzsche himself had given instructions should be destroyed.

The similar case of Franz Kafka is instructive. His greatest creations - *The Trial*, *Metamorphosis* and *The Castle* - would all have been consigned to the flames had his friend Max

Brod obeyed their author's dying wish. Yet Brod was a gifted novelist and critic in his own right who wanted nothing more than for his friend's talents to be acknowledged. Elisabeth had little of the intellectual sympathy with Nietzsche's work that Brod had with Kafka's. Rudolf Steiner was shocked when he first met Elisabeth by how little understanding of her brother's thought she had. He offered to tutor her, an offer the keeper of the archive duly accepted. This doesn't mean to imply that she had any less understanding of his philosophy than many of his first disciples but it is hard to see Elisabeth's motives as altruistic. Förster-Nietzsche was a rabid anti-Semite with a decidedly lackadaisical approach to what constituted a text by her brother. It is difficult not to be suspicious of the inclusion of fragments that Nietzsche, a man who thrived on jotting down his ideas at will and then revising at length, had so readily discarded. It would, however, be her views on race that would do most to make his name associated with what Nietzsche calls, in *Ecce Homo*, 'something frightful- of a crisis like no other before on earth.'

Nietzsche Nazi?

'Deutschland, Deutschland über Alles was, I fear, the end of German philosophy.'

Nietzsche, *Twilight of the Idols*

'I had so often sung Deutschland über Alles and so often roared 'Heil' that I now thought it was as a kind of retro-active grace that I was granted the right of appearing before the Court of Eternal Justice to testify to the truth of those sentiments.'

Adolf Hitler, *Mein Kampf*

In the Nuremberg war trials of 1946 it was claimed that Nietzsche's philosophy had been central to Nazi ideology. Yet as we have already seen Nietzsche had little truck with both the nation of his birth, preferring to consider himself Polish, and with anti-Semitism. Unfortunately the bowdlerised version of his thought peddled by his sister in *The Will to Power* led many to believe he had a different opinion. Shorn of their context and more often than not arranged in such a way as to favour Elisabeth's own crude racist views, many of his bombastic pronouncements about supermen and noble races do appear distinctly fascistic. Nietzsche is elitist and at times, by our standards, racist. Unequivocal condemnation, however, is not always easy with Nietzsche. It might appear difficult to find any justification for a statement like, 'One would no more choose to associate with first Christians than one would with Polish Jews... Neither of them smell very nice.' Yet it appears in *The Anti-Christ*. However, if we consider that in his next book *Ecce Homo* he explicitly associates his sense of smell with gaining knowledge, it is easier to see that the statement should not necessarily be taken at face value. Nietzsche is sniffing out hypocrisy in religion as a whole not just throwing racist insults around. Nietzsche's style, with its stress on short, provocative and even contradictory statements, made him an easy target for appropriation. We have only to consider the fact that his 'blond beast', symbolising a lion, found itself providing justification for a fairhaired Germanic master race to realise how biased Nazi readings of his works were.

Nietzsche had nothing but contempt for what he called the herd mentality and this is usually taken as a sign that he would have favoured the eradication of lesser mortals. Given his hated for the slavish values of Bismarck's Second Reich there is absolutely nothing to suggest he would have liked the mass mentality of the Third Reich any more for just the same reason. Nietzsche believed that, since Socrates, all political systems had developed along slavish lines. He wanted to see a re-emergence of strong, aristocratic values and it is difficult to imagine that he would have found them amongst the Nazis. That Elisabeth felt qualified to announce in 1935 that she had no doubt that Adolf Hitler was the Superman foretold by Zarathustra proves how little understanding of her brother's work she really had. Hitler and the Nazis clearly relished and used many of Nietzsche's remarks about the need for war, strength and ruthlessness for their own ends. However, as they co-opted material from sources as varied as Arthurian legends and the pseudo- sciences to justify their dogma, it is distinctly unfair and insulting to blame Nietzsche - a man who had spent a good deal of his life railing against anti-Semites, the German state and Wagner's Germanic myths - for their atrocities.

Sigmund

Born when Nietzsche was twelve, Sigmund Freud is often seen as one of the most important inheritors of his sceptical method. Freud himself claimed to have been anticipated, though not influenced, by Nietzsche. He described Nietzsche as 'a philosopher whose guesses and intuitions often agree in the most astonishing way with the laborious findings of psychoanalysis.' In fact they both share a common mentor in Arthur Schopenhauer. The Danzig depressive was widely read and discussed in Vienna, Freud's home for most of his life, and his theory of the ever-striving will seems to have influenced Freud's theory of the Id, the instinctive impulse of the unconscious.

Both Nietzsche and Freud can be said to have been interested in exploring what Karl Marx termed 'false consciousness'. Marx had argued that people believe they think freely when actually their ideas are conditioned by the ruling classes. Nietzsche turned this on its head by claiming that in fact it was the herd who nobbled and crippled the free or aristocratic spirits and not the other way round. But while Nietzsche revelled in the irrational Freud saw the dangers. He accepted, like Nietzsche, that man was not rational, at least in the Enlightenment sense of the word, and was driven by inner forces. The mind is capable of mental activity that is independent of consciousness and strives to defend itself by constructively forgetting experiences and urges. In *Human, All Too Human* and *The Genealogy of Morals* Nietzsche argued that even acts we believe to be benevolent and selfless have very different, sublimated motivations behind them. Freud too believed that we spend our entire lives deceiving both others and ourselves as to the real reasons behind our actions. For Freud though this was done to avoid confronting the truth about the feelings of lust and murder we all harbour towards our parents. These were dangerous, even Dionysian desires and, while Freud felt it was essential to understand them by undergoing analysis, he firmly believed that irrationality must be regulated in the interests of human society. His position, though quite at odds with much of Nietzsche's later thought with its jamboree of irrationality, has striking parallels with *The Birth of Tragedy*.

Nietzsche's Dionysus, the primary and sensual side of human nature, and the Apollinian, its civilising rational counterpart, are virtually synonymous with Freud's Id and Ego. The Greeks, Nietzsche maintained, had been able to cope with existence by mediating the raw horrors of the Dionysian through the Apollinian but, after Socrates, the Dionysian part of our natures was 'repressed' and, as a result, man had become sick. Freud's psychoanalytic 'cure' could almost be seen as a way of redressing the balance by making us more aware of our true natures. He too saw the conflict between our instincts and the requirements of civilisation as harmful but, unlike Nietzsche, he felt they were an unavoidable part of human existence. Human beings are for Freud, as for Hobbes and Nietzsche, aggressive by nature. Society, through the family, church and government forces us to submit our individual desires to the good of the group. We feel anxious and frustrated because our true desires are not met. If we attempt to break the rules though we feel guilt. The result either way is neurosis. We all suffer from it but some are able to cope better than others. The latter require therapy but even the former will use religion, drugs, politics, sex and food as crutches to sustain themselves, all the while never succeeding in becoming fully human. Civilisation is a tremendous burden but, for Freud the alternative - unfettered individualism - would be far worse. Nietzsche would have found this pessimistic conclusion unacceptable. He would rather will the irrational than submit to restraints that hinder the individual. 'Happiness and instinct' he states in *Twilight of the Idols*, 'are one' as long as life is ascending. To 'have to combat one's instincts that is the formula for decadence.'

What A Novel Idea

Few philosophers have had as much direct influence on literature as Nietzsche. His success with writers in the early part of twentieth century can largely be attributed to his critique of the prevailing morality rather than any specific doctrine. One of the first novelists to be inspired by Nietzsche's rejection of bourgeois mediocrity was Andre Gide. His 1902 novel

The Immoralist is awash with Nietzschean themes. The book follows Michel, a young classicist on a journey of self-fulfilment. Michel, raised in a strict protestant family, marries Marceline, a woman he does not love to appease his father. On their honeymoon in north Africa he becomes ill. Faced with his own mortality he realises he has never done what he truly wanted to and vows, from now on, to follow the promptings of his inner being rather than conform to custom. He makes love to his wife for the first time, seeks pleasure with the local Arab boys and builds up his formerly weedy body with exercise. He begins to feel nothing but contempt for the weak. When his pious wife suffers a miscarriage while he is cavorting with a male friend and begins to sicken he refuses to indulge in hypocritical pity. Gide's attitude to his malevolent hero is loosely equivalent to his attitude to Nietzsche. Though the novel is largely autobiographical - Gide like Michel, had an extremely Puritanical upbringing, his marriage to his cousin Madelaine Rondeaux remained unconsummated and he'd had his first homosexual experiences in north Africa - he views Michel as a destructive, nihilistic force. He believed that Nietzsche's views were extremely useful but too dangerous to be propagated unmediated.

In England where Nietzsche's work first appeared in 1900 he was enthusiastically embraced by the Fabian society, an eclectic socialist group who campaigned for equal rights for the working classes and the emancipation of women. George Bernard Shaw was a prominent member and in 1903 he wrote *Man and Superman*, a philosophical comedy that managed to combine his own form of socialism individualism with Nietzsche's Übermensch in a deft retelling of Don Juan. Shaw like many of the Fabians was also a keen advocate of eugenics. In Edwardian England eugenics, the 'science' of improved breeding first formulated by the explorer and anthropologist Sir Francis Galton in his 1856 book *Hereditary Genius,* was widely discussed and even accepted by people from both ends of the political spectrum. Nietzsche was erroneously believed to provide further intellectual muscle to the cause.

D.H. Lawrence, after discovering *The Will to Power* in Croydon public library in 1908, was so taken by its claim that the 'great majority of men have no right to existence' that he proposed building a 'lethal chamber as big as Crystal Palace' into which he would lead all 'the sick, the halt and the maimed' while a brass band pumped out the Hallelujah Chorus. (Tubercular teacher novelists were obviously not deemed sick.) This crude interpretation aside, Nietzsche's writings had a profound effect on Lawrence. In *Twilight in Italy,* his 1916 travel narrative, he contrasts, in much the same way that Nietzsche did in *The Gay Science,* the pagan free spirits of the Italian peasants with the cold Christian north. The novels *Aaron's Rod* and *Kangaroo* both make use of the ideas of the Superman and the Will to Power.

It would, however, be in the novels of two Germans, Thomas Mann and Herman Hesse that Nietzsche's ideas would receive, at least artistically, their fullest exposition. For Mann the culmination of his lifetime engagement with Nietzsche's thought occurs in *Doctor Faustus,* arguably his masterwork. In this he explores the themes of genius and madness by dramatising many of the events, most notably the visit to the Cologne brothel, of Nietzsche's life. He parallels the downfall of Germany at the end of the Second World War with the mental collapse of the diabolic composer Adrian Leverkûhn, a truly Nietzschean figure. The connection between sickness and the artistic spirit is made time and time again in his novels. In *Buddenbrooks* he explores decay and decadence and

The Magic Mountain, its title taken from *The Birth of Tragedy*, is a powerful allegory of a subject central to Nietzschean thought - the sickness of European civilisation. The inhabitants of the book's lofty sanatorium spend their days 'sitting out' existence, discussing a world from which they are physically removed. Their essential but selfish convalescence mirrors the work of the artist who, in Mann's and Nietzsche's view, stands apart from society. The book also explores Nietzsche's idea of the eternal recurrence. The entire life of the novel's community is based on a circular, repetitive daily routine and the book itself mimics this to produce a profound meditation on the nature of time. In one chapter the central character Hans Castrop becomes lost in a snowdrift after skiing in circles. Faced with an unending array of identical, blurry whiteness, he realises he stands between ignoring an icy death or being consumed by it. He decides, in true Übermensch fashion, that for 'the sake of goodness and love' he 'shall let death have no more sovereignty over his thoughts.' To live gallantly, affirming existence is the only option.

Herman Hesse, like Nietzsche, was expected to follow in his father's footsteps and become a Protestant pastor. He too rebelled, working as a bookseller, antique dealer and mechanic whilst starting to write and became a full-time writer after his first book *Peter Camenzind* was published in 1904. At the outbreak of the First World War Hesse was so appalled by the prevailing mood of militarism and nationalism that he moved to Switzerland. Here he spent his time attacking German patriotism. In 1919, just after the war, Hesse published *Zarathustra's Return*, a study of Nietzsche, and the novel *Demian*, a Freudian study of incest with a distinctly Nietzschean slant. Hesse saw the need for self-realisation as the primary goal of human existence and in *Siddhartha* and *Steppenwolf* he examined the conflict between the demands of bourgeois society and achieving this aim, taking a steer from Eastern philosophy and some of Nietzsche's more Dionysian claims. It was in his final book, *The Glass Bead Game*, that he drew most heavily on Nietzsche. Set in the 23rd Century in a mountain kingdom where an intellectual elite has flourished, the novel pays homage to many of the ideals for emancipating the human spirit that Nietzsche had explored in *The Gay Science* and *Thus Spoke Zarathustra*. The fate of Josef Knecht, the novel's central character even mirrors that of Zarathustra. He leaves his serene retreat to go down among men and drowns.

The Existentialists

It is almost impossible to imagine Existentialism without Nietzsche. However, although some of his preoccupations - irrationality, dread, suffering and moral hypocrisy - are very similar to those of the leading Existentialists it would be a mistake to regard Nietzsche as an Existentialist thinker. Jean-Paul Sartre, following on from Karl Jaspers and Martin Heidegger, defined the first principle of Existentialism as that 'existence precedes essence.' Man is nothing at birth, human identity is not fixed and we must actively choose what we want to become. At the heart of this is free 'will', much akin to Nietzsche's idea of will, that can determine our actions. For Sartre the first dreadful fact is that of our existence. From this we come to realise that we are free and thus condemned to make choices. There is no God and there are no other crutches on which we can lean. We are utterly adrift at the mercy of our own freedom. To live authentically, for the Existentialists (as in a way it was for Nietzsche), is to accept human existence in the face of this terrible truth. Albert Camus, in a passage that echoes Nietzsche, imagined Sisyphus, who in Greek mythology is compelled to roll a rock up a hill for eternity, as happy. For 'the absurd man… who knows himself to be master of his days… says yes.' Because 'the universe henceforth without a master seems to him neither sterile nor futile.' The idea that men must accept their place in the material world without recourse to transcendent values and that they must live as if there is nothing beyond life is certainly drawn from Nietzsche. Sartre in his childhood memoir *Words* even speaks of his *légèreté* or lightness, an inability to take himself seriously, a word which could easily be at home in *The Gay Science*. However, for all their similarities, Nietzsche's stoical but joyous acceptance of fate seems at odds with Existentialism's rejection of human nature. Nietzsche wanted to remove the false crutches of the Judaeo-Christian faith precisely because they impeded true human nature; which is quite different from claiming that no such thing exists. Nietzsche, as we have seen, held fairly reactionary ideas about quite who would be capable of achieving his higher state of being and felt in his own time that no-one had yet reached such a level because even the greatest men were all-too-human. The Existentialists appear to argue that an authenticity should be available to anyone who is able to grasp his or her freedom. These quibbles aside, Nietzsche's Will to Power is a fundamental if sublimated tenet of Existentialism. For Sartre, human relations are intrinsically antagonistic. Caught in the gaze of another human we struggle to prevent them from turning us from a free being into an object and we do this by attempting to capture the consciousness of another by making the other an object. When the other is an object for us our freedom returns, because nothing is an object for an object. While we are attempting to free ourselves from the hold of the other, however, the other is attempting to do exactly the same thing. As

Sartre puts it while we 'seek to enslave the Other, the Other seeks to enslave us.' 'Conflict', he concludes, 'is the original meaning of being-for-others.'

Wittgenstein

Ludwig Wittgenstein, who as an adult took great delight in placing Schopenhauer's (by then deeply unfashionable) tomes on the empty shelves of his Cambridge rooms, was raised in an affluent and intellectually voracious Viennese family. Wittgenstein, who went to school with a more notorious fan of Nietzsche, Adolf Hitler, would certainly have been aware, if only indirectly, of many of Nietzsche's ideas from quite a young age. It's striking how similar, both in method, style and interests, Wittgenstein's later philosophy is to Nietzsche's. Like his Prussian neighbour, the mature Wittgenstein was a radical sceptic in the vein of the ancient Greeks. Both thinkers dance around problems, defying final judgements. Wittgenstein's notebooks and lectures, published posthumously in the Philosophical Investigations and the Blue and the Brown Books, rely, much as Nietzsche's writings do, on short provocative statements that invite the reader to engage with the text. They are often no more than hints or clues. He did not believe that there was an external or eternal justification for the meaning of our words, meaning could only be defined in terms of use. Language is a human invention and only has value in its practical effects. Human relationships are finite and therefore need acknowledgement, not justification and proof. A language arises from 'a form of life'. What we take to be literal expressions are not truths but a complex web of metaphors and similes that, over time, we have ceased to regard as figurative. Nietzsche too argued that what we thought of as truths were in fact illusions whose illu-

81

sory nature had been forgotten. In an early essay - written over fifty years before Wittgenstein had come to the same conclusion - he pondered: 'So what is truth? A mobile army of metaphors, metonyms, anthropomorphisms - in short an aggregate of human relationships.' The job of philosophy, Wittgenstein maintains (in a phrase that could easily be attributed to Nietzsche) was not to uncover truth but 'to destroy idols. 'And', he adds, 'that does not mean creating new ones.' In another statement that Friedrich would certainly have approved of, he claimed that 'one should write philosophy only as one writes a poem.'

The Umbrellas Of Naumburg - Postmodernism

Even though the word postmodernism or post-modernism was first used by the British artist John Watkins when Nietzsche was alive and relatively well and living in Basel, it is Nietzsche that is usually credited with being the father or even grandfather of post-modernism. Given that the term itself is somewhat amorphous - a refuge for post-Marxist French intellectuals, American liberal ironists and radical global capitalists - most commentators are split between arguing that Nietzsche was either its first practitioner or that post-modernism was just the kind of thing that he would have denounced as decadent. In a sense both positions (if we ourselves are going to be postmodern) are equally valid interpretations. For, while Nietzsche was the first philosopher to call into question the legitimacy of objective truth, a distinctly postmodern outlook, many of the solutions he offers are dogmatic, elitist and distinctly un-postmodern.

Nietzsche's figurative style, as we have seen, lends itself to all manner of readings and interpretations and has both influenced postmodernists like Jacques Derrida and allowed them to select, like earlier and perhaps less benign readers, material to favour their own views. For postmodernists a text can never have one final meaning - a point that Nietzsche himself made in *The Will to Power* where he claimed there were no facts 'only interpretations' - because all writers use language, a collection of arbitrary signs. Language is seen by most postmodernists as a matter of convention. It doesn't correspond to the 'real' world but is a self-contained system that only refers and relates to itself. As such all our thoughts are trapped by it, so all bold claims to objective knowledge are false. For Nietzsche, too, the notion of the truth of a statement is irrelevant. The 'question is to what extent is it life-advancing, life-preserving'. Claims to truth are useful fictions and he writes that, 'without falsification of the world by numbers, mankind could not live'. He adds that to 'renounce false judgements would be to renounce life.' What we must do, however, is to recognise, paradoxically, 'untruth as a condition of life.' If god is dead so too are the grand meta-narratives of philosophy, science and religion. On the downside this means that Nietzsche's own system is equally vulnerable. For the postmodernists it is precisely this that makes Nietzsche so interesting.

Jacques Derrida

Though the French-Algerian philosopher Jacques Derrida argues there is no such thing as the truth of Nietzsche or of his texts, he is clearly a child of and practitioner of Nietzsche's Joyful Wisdom. He is, if this were possible, even more sceptical than Nietzsche was. Though untruth for Nietzsche is a painful but pragmatic 'fact', he clearly believed that some 'truths' were of greater value than others i.e. that they were more life-affirming. Nietzsche's genealogical method aimed at revealing the life-denying hidden origins of ethical, moral and metaphysical judgements. Derrida, on the other hand, does not believe in meaning. His project is not to offer up preferential interpretations but to show the inherent instability of meaning. Deconstruction, his non-methodical method for doing this, is not a thesis or set of beliefs but a way of reading texts, usually philosophical ones. Its aim is simply to show that these texts do not mean what they seem to mean, do not mean what their authors intended them to mean and in fact do not have any conclusive meaning at all. This is because all philosophers' attempts to get at the truth are thwarted by the very language they use. They are unable to get beyond language and their works are riddled with linguistic tensions and contradictions which end up subverting their stated goals and their claims to truth.

Deconstructive readings show up the semantic inconsistencies in these texts by revealing how certain ideas are privileged. For Derrida we know that 'dear' is different from 'bear' not because they are connected to the world but because they look and sound different in our system of signs. We construct meaning from these differences. Language is slippery stuff, however, so when we write or speak, some of these differences will be given preferential treatment over others whose meanings will be 'deferred'. Thus there is no stable relationship between a philosopher and reader or even a speaker and a listener, as what are thought to be univocal statements are just, to quote Nietzsche, 'a mobile army of metaphors'. Derrida calls into question the whole of western metaphysics, although, unlike Nietzsche, he is much less worried about producing anything to replace it. One of the major criticisms of deconstruction is that it is always a parasitic activity, criticising other works but not producing a new non-essentialist philosophy. However, for Derrida, this looks impossible because all language is metaphorical and to even attempt to try would be folly. He instead extols Nietzsche's 'playful innocence of becoming'.

Derrida's trouncing of what he calls logocentrism, western philosophy's habit of positing a rational language that perfectly represents the world, owes a fair bit to Nietzsche's scepticism but as the Prussian thinker said one repays a teacher badly by remaining a pupil. In *Spurs* Derrida deconstructed Nietzsche. He revealed not only the origins of his own deconstructive method but also a curious feminist streak to the philosopher usually regarded as a rabid misogynist. Nietzsche repeatedly associates women with wily sirens who lure the male philosophers from their path. If an idea becomes more subtle, insidious and incomprehensible, he maintains 'it becomes female.' Yet it is precisely this kind of 'insidious' destruction of philosophy that Nietzsche is himself engaged in. His misogynist rants belie a deferred range of interpretations. The 'same' words can signify their exact opposite and correspond to an inverted meaning. He spurns woman but is also spurred on by them to destroy the monoliths of philosophy so he can be seen as far more ambivalent about woman than is usually supposed. He can even be seen as a crypto-feminist. These competing versions of Nietzsche arise from the syntax and logic of his writings but none can be said to articulate the absolute truth of Nietzsche. In a rather playful and provocative aside Derrida argues that even a note from Nietzsche saying 'I have forgotten my umbrella' is just as relevant/irrelevant as anything else he wrote because there can never be a true Nietzsche. There are only texts that we can read. You can't help feeling that even Nietzsche would have balked at such an idea.

Michel Foucault

Michel Foucault is perhaps the greatest heir to Nietzsche's genealogical method. Foucault, who studied and taught in a Marxist Liberal tradition of French academia, found Nietzsche's reflections on power and the nature of knowledge deeply liberating and embarked on what he called his 'archaeology' of modern thought.

Nietzsche was fundamentally opposed to histories that claimed to reveal an eternal truth. He argued, in 'On the Uses and Disadvantages of History for Life', and elsewhere that effective history would only be able to evade the shadow of such metaphysical speculation by realising that everything previously thought to be immortal must be placed within history. Knowledge was a human project and as such histories of love, cruelty and punishment and the gritty realities of human existence were more worthwhile than grand narratives that attempted to reveal non-existent eternal truths. Foucault effectively fulfilled Nietzsche's wish by writing a series of micro-histories that all attempted to understand a key concern of Nietzsche's: the nature of power.

In the late 1960s Foucault began to feel that the Marxist or sociological interpretations of power, which tended to define it in purely economic or prohibitive terms, were too simplistic. Such political philosophy seemed to assume that power was a metaphysical entity that states could take control of rather than something that arose from a complex web of human interactions. Like Nietzsche he believed that knowledge and power were virtually inseparable and that what we take to be truths are actually expedient cultural fictions. Power couldn't therefore just be repressive. It must permeate every facet of existence. It is something we live rather than possess and, as such, the notion of power and the way it manifests itself changes as culture develops. Just as our language is really a collection of long-forgotten metaphors, our social rules are based on a web of power structures we are unaware of, the roots of which stretch back into history. In his studies of punishment, madness and sexuality Foucault uncovered the suppressed and unconscious facets of history. By exploring what the dominant social order choose to exclude or disqualify he argued you discover what is legitimised as knowledge and truth and what isn't. At the time of the Enlightenment, when reason became dominant, a whole range of social categories such as the criminal, mad and deviant were created to define that which was not deemed rational. Traditional ways of speaking about power in terms of repression/liberation are equally part of this process so, for Foucault, they fail to tell us anything profound. There can never be an overarching history. There are only ever a multitude of overlapping narratives, some of which are legitimised and others excluded. His work, much like Nietzsche's was concerned with showing the historical contingency of what we take to be the truth. Foucault can be seen as exemplifying the kind of perspectivism that is often deemed to have begun with Nietzsche.

In Foucault's *History of Sexuality* we find even more overt signs of Nietzsche's influence. In this work he begins his analysis of our idea of sexuality by contrasting it with Ancient Greek culture. He argues that our notion of sexuality would have been incomprehensible to them. The Greeks, he claims did not have a single moral code. Instead sexual conduct was stipulated by social position. Sexual acts were, therefore, not in themselves wrong but were only judged inappropriate if they were perceived to be excessive. Self-mastery and moderation were at the heart of their sexual ethics. Christianity changed that by condemning sexual acts and making desire itself the subject of ethical speculation. This radically transformed subjective experience. Every inner desire could now be held up and examined against a universal ethical code. For Foucault, as it was for Nietzsche and Freud, the conscience is the internalised version of this code and it became institutionalised in the Confession. By the Victorian era, however, scientific discourse began to replace religion and sexuality became categorised according to scientific knowledge. What previously had been condemned as 'bad acts' were now used to define types of individuals that could be cured. Sexuality became a way of defining identity and knowledge of what was normal sexuality also became a way of exerting power. Just as Nietzsche was sceptical of science replacing religion so Foucault argues that psychoanalysis looks remarkably similar to, and serves the same function as, the confessional. We should try to remember that even sexual identity, something many would like to pretend is self-evidently true, is just the product of certain historical and cultural ways of describing subjectivity and that what is really at issue is power. While clearly Foucault inherits much of Nietzsche's genealogy, it is his intent to unmask the insidious notion of truth that makes him, perhaps, of all recent philosophers, the one closest to Nietzsche's aims.

6. Further Reading

Works

Nietzsche's Major Works with dates of original publication in German:

The Birth of Tragedy (1872)
Untimely Meditations Part 1 (1873)
Untimely Meditations Part 2 (1874)
Untimely Meditations Part 3 (1874)
Untimely Meditations Part 4 (1876)
Human, All Too Human (1878)
Human, All Too Human: Assorted Opinions and Sayings (1879)
Human, All Too Human: The Wanderer and his Shadow (1880)
Daybreak (1881)
The Gay Science Parts 1-4 (1882)
The Gay Science Part 5 (1887)
Thus Spake Zarathustra (1883-86)
Beyond Good and Evil (1886)
On the Genealogy of Morals (1887)
The Case of Wagner (1888)
Twilight of the Idols (1888)
Nietzsche Contra Wagner (1888)
The Anti-Christ (1888)
Ecce Homo (1888)

There are various different editions of almost all of Nietzsche's individual works in English translation. Most are currently in print and the major works can be bought cheaply in Penguin, Oxford and Hackett editions. For those readers wanting to get an overview of Nietzsche's rich oeuvre though there are two handy and reasonably priced compendiums well worth purchasing.

They are *A Nietzsche Reader* ed. R.G Hollingdale Penguin 1977 £7.99 and *The Portable Nietzsche* ed. Walter Kaufmann Viking 1954. Hollingdale's reader arranges extracts from most of Nietzsche's writings into themed chapters covering such thorny issues as morality, the superman and the will to power. Kaufmann's book contains *Thus Spoke Zarathustra*, *Twilight of the Idols*, *The Antichrist* and *Nietzsche contra Wagner* plus a range of other pieces.

Commentaries

A Very Short Introduction to Nietzsche by Michael Tanner OUP new ed. 2000 (formerly the 1993 Past Master)
   As it says on the tin this compact introduction from Cambridge don and Wagner biographer Tanner offers a short, sharp and even occasionally testy tour of Nietzsche's philosophy.

Nietzsche: A Critical Reader ed. Peter Sedgwick Blackwell £17.99
   Engaging and reasonably accessible, this offers some helpful interpretations of Nietzsche's texts and some of the issues they raise.

Nietzsche: Philosopher, Psychologist and Antichrist by Walter Kaufmann Princeton University Press 1974
   Though Kaufmann's reputation has suffered in recent years-most commentators now find his claims that Nietzsche was a liberal humanist unconvincing- this seminal work is well worth reading.

Nietzsche's Philosophy of Art by Julian Young CUP 1992
   A scholarly but engaging study of Nietzsche's aesthetics, Young's book also offers an intriguing exploration of Schopenhauer's influence.

Nietzsche and Philosophy by A.C Danto Columbia University Press 1965
   Arthur Danto's sober but sympathetic book is one of the most

convincing attempts to offer a systematic account of Nietzsche's thought.

Nietzsche: Life as Literature by A Nehemas Harvard University Press 1985

A more modern or perhaps more accurately post-modern analysis of Nietzsche's work can be found in Nehemas' engaging book.

The New Nietzsche ed. D Allison MIT Press 1985

For the more adventurous this collection offers readings from the likes of such contemporary continental thinkers as Jacques Derrida and Gilles Deleuze.

Biographies

Nietzsche

Selected Letters of Friedrich Nietzsche ed. Christopher Middleton Hackett 1996 Hackett

This draws together over two hundred of Nietzsche's letters, including his correspondence with Richard Wagner, Lou Salome, his mother and his notorious sister. It provides an insight into the formation of many of his ideas and, as the books progresses, his growing sense of isolation and ultimately his insanity.

Conversations with Nietzsche ed. Gilman Sander OUP £16.95

A fascinating collection of memoirs, anecdotes and recollections from some of Nietzsche's contemporaries.

The Tragic Philosopher by F Lea Athlone Press 1993

Although originally published in the 1950s Lea's book is a still a highly readable account of Nietzsche's life.

Nietzsche: A Critical Life by Ronald Hayman 1980 Weidenfeld and Nicolson £12.99

A comprehensive and compelling biography that offers many informative comments on his philosophy.

Nietzsche in Turin: The End of the Future by Lesley Chamberlain Quartet 1996 £7

This absolutely charming book offers a rich portrait of Nietzsche in his final year of sanity. Full of enchanting insights and conjectures, Chamberlain provides an extremely moving and passionate defence of Nietzsche the man and the thinker. Highly recommended.

Lou Salome

Looking Back: The Intimate Friendships with Nietzsche, Rilke & Freud by Lou Andreas-Salome Paragon 1998 £13.50

The inimitable Lou's own account of her extraordinary life.

Frau Lou: Nietzsche's Wayward Disciple by Rudolph Binion Princeton 1968

This is, unfortunately, now out of print but can be found second hand.

Elisabeth Förster- Nietzsche

The Young Nietzsche by Elisabeth Förster- Nietzsche London 1912

The Lonely Nietzsche by Elisabeth Förster- Nietzsche London 1915

Both of Elisabeth's self-aggrandising accounts of Nietzsche's life are out of print.

Forgotten Fatherland : The Search for Elisabeth Nietzsche by Ben MacIntyre Farrar Straus & Giroux 1992

MacIntyre travelled to Paraguay to see what remained of Förster-Nietzsche's Nueva Germania colony. The resulting book, part travelogue, part biography, is a riveting exploration of the damage Elisabeth and her husband wreaked on the colony and her brother's reputation.

Wagner

Wagner by Michael Tanner Fontana 1995 £6.99

Tanner's study of Wagner has its detractors but for a short, accessible and engaging examination of his life and music few better it.

Wagner and Philosophy by Bryan Magee Allen Lane 2000 £20.00

This recent book from Magee traces the composer's philosophical development, or deterioration depending on your point of view, and deals at length with the Wagner-Nietzsche friendship.

Schopenhauer

Schopenhauer and The Wild Years of Philosophy by Rudiger Safranski Weidenfeld 1989

Staggeringly good and unfortunately out of print biography of the misanthropic thinker who profoundly influenced Nietzsche and Wagner. Well worth trawling your local or not so local second hand book emporium for.

The Philosophy of Schopenhauer Bryan Magee OUP 15.99 New Ed 1997

A solid introduction to Schopenhauer, packed with interesting biographical details and cogent analysis of his philosophy.

Websites

http://www.cwu.edu/~millerj/nietzsche/ - The Pirate Nietzsche site is a veritable feast of Nietzsche texts, facts, articles and ephemera.

http://www.inquiria.com/nz/index.html - Nietzsche's Labyrinth. With several out of copyright translations of Nietzsche's works to download and swathes of articles, this somewhat gothic looking site is well worth logging on to.

http://infonectar.com/aphorisms.html - The self explanatory Nietzsche Aphorism Page offers a nugget of Nietzsche wisdom at the click of a mouse.

http://www.fns.org.uk/index.htm - The Friedrich Nietzsche Society was formed in 1990 to, in their own words, 'promote the study of the life, work and influence of Friedrich Nietzsche.' You can find out what they are up to and even join through this site.

http://www.pitt.edu/~wbcurry/nietzsche.html - The Perspectives of Nietzsche. This has a fine selection of Nietzsche quotes and short extracts arranged by theme.

http://www.rensselaer.edu/~macphm/Nietzsche/ - The Nietzsche Center, (yes it's American) has a number of stimulating essays and a quite wonderful graded links page. One site listed is helpfully described as 'being found to contain grossly inaccurate and poorly interpreted material.'

The Essential Library

New This Month:

Sergio Leone (£3.99)   Spaghetti Westerns (£3.99)
Nietzsche (£3.99)

New Next Month:

Steven Spielberg (£3.99)   Feminism (£3.99)
Sherlock Holmes (£3.99)   Alchemists & Alchemy (£3.99)

Film Directors:

Jane Campion (£2.99)   John Carpenter (£3.99)
Jackie Chan (£2.99)   Joel & Ethan Coen (£2.99)
David Cronenberg (£3.99)   Terry Gilliam (£2.99)
Alfred Hitchcock (£2.99)   Krzysztof Kieslowski (£2.99)
Stanley Kubrick (£2.99)   David Lynch (£3.99)
Brian De Palma (£2.99)   Sam Peckinpah (£2.99)
Ridley Scott (£3.99)   Orson Welles (£2.99)
Billy Wilder (£3.99)

Film Genres:

Film Noir (£3.99)   Heroic Bloodshed (£2.99)
Horror Films (£3.99)   Slasher Movies(£3.99)
Vampire Films (£2.99)

Miscellaneous Film Subjects:

Steve McQueen (£2.99)   Marilyn Monroe (£3.99)
The Oscars® (£3.99)   Filming On A Microbudget (£3.99)

TV:

Doctor Who (£3.99)

Books:

Cyberpunk (£3.99)   Philip K Dick (£3.99)
Hitchhiker's Guide (£3.99)   Noir Fiction (£2.99)
Terry Pratchett (£3.99)

Ideas:

Conspiracy Theories (£3.99)

Available at all good bookstores, or send a cheque to: **Pocket Essentials (Dept NZ), 18 Coleswood Rd, Harpenden, Herts, AL5 1EQ, UK**. Please make cheques payable to 'Oldcastle Books.' Add 50p postage & packing for each book in the UK and £1 elsewhere.

US customers can send $6.95 plus $1.95 postage & packing for each book to: **Trafalgar Square Publishing, PO Box 257, Howe Hill Road, North Pomfret, Vermont 05053, USA**. e-mail: tsquare@sover.net

Customers worldwide can order online at **www.pocketessentials.com**.